A Book I Wrote

Toby Nix

Loudermilk Publishing LLC

Back cover author photo by Beth Neely

Dedication

This book is for my mother. She instilled a love for reading in me at a very early age. She read books to me until I was able to read, at which point she would sit and listen to me read books to her. We read the same books to each other no telling how many times. "The Berenstain bears", "Amelia Bedelia" and "Encyclopedia Brown" accounted for at least 90% of all our reading time. As I got older I discovered Judy Blume, and "SuperFudge" and found another book I could read over and over.

She drove me to Pizza Hut to get my personal pan pizza when I had read whatever the "Book It" requirements were to get a free pizza.

She is my biggest fan and if we are going by what she says, all my columns are gold. I'm fine with her assessment, biased as it may be.

Introduction

If you are reading this introduction, you bought my second book. Either that or you stole it. Or maybe I gave it to you. I don't know.

My first book, "Columns I wrote" came out last year and did better than I was hoping it would do. I haven't been able to quit my day job yet and I never appeared on the New York Times best seller list, but I was able to take the family to the beach on "book money" so I'll take it.

The weirdest thing for me about my first book was coming to terms with the fact that people wanted me to sign the book. A few even asked me if I charged extra for signing it. That made for several awkward moments for me, and more than several awkward signatures.

It's weird to think people want your signature on something. It's an awesome feeling, but it took some getting used to.

If you bought that first book and I wrote something ridiculously awkward in it, forgive me. I hope I will do better this time around, if I am given a second chance at signing.

This book contains every newspaper column I wrote in 2018, preceded by four previously unpublished writings. The unpublished writings are from a collection of mine I've been sitting on for several years. It's tough to "put yourself out there." I think I'm a better writer now, than when I wrote these first four chapters. They are raw, but they are real and I wrote them.

Some of these were more emotional than others to write. I hope you enjoy at least a couple.

OLD TIME RELIGION

I didn't grow up in the church. I think that puts me in the minority as a southern child of the 80's. I grew up believing in God, Jesus and all that the Bible taught, without ever really questioning any of it. My parents, along with almost everyone around me spoke of it all as if it were true, so there was no need for me to question any of it.

Once in a blue moon, I can remember my mom dragging me against my will to church. I know I got very little out of any service I was ever forced to attend. I was able to take my working knowledge of watched pots never boiling and transfer it over to a stared at wristwatch never advances.

I learned how to lip sync, although I don't think it was called lip syncing back then. This was before Milli Vanilli made it famous and before most modern musicians made it the norm. I would stand up, holding my hymnal, turned to the correct page and move my mouth along with the words that were being sung.

I would have been terrified for anyone to hear me singing back then, but I always felt the Preacher and the entire choir were 100% fixated on me, judging whether or not I was singing, so I pretended to sing along.

My facial expression never moved, only my lips. Even if the choir was staring at me, as I assumed they were, they must have thought I sang like Ben Stein speaks. Ma used to give me either a handful of quarters or a couple of dollars to put in the offering plate. I did enjoy that part of the service, reaching in to my pockets and digging out a little money and nonchalantly tossing it in the offering plate as if I were a big shot.

Once the actual sermon started, I was usually tuned out and staring at my wristwatch within a matter of minutes. It felt like minutes, it was probably more like seconds. I never even made it to where I was supposed to flip to the scripture to read along with the Preacher. I didn't see the point in reading along with him if he was going to tell me what it said and then tell me what it meant to boot. Even when I went to church as a teenager, and then an adult I could never follow along very well with the sermon.

Outside of the offering portion of the service, I was also always intrigued with the communion service. A male, other than the Preacher, would come to the pulpit up and give a three to four minute speech on the importance of communion. He would then say a prayer and pass out trays of bread (tiny crackers) and trays filled with little glasses of grape juice for all the Christians to take. It was always more somber than anything else, which pulled me in. I was also always excluded from it, which really pulled me in! What was this they were drinking and eating and why wasn't I allowed to partake?

Surely it was this kind of temptation that led Eve to try the forbidden fruit and put us all in these uncomfortable pews in the first place. Nothing looks better than something you can't have, and each time I was drug into church, here was a little plate of crackers and tiny cups of grape juice being paraded right in front of my face that I couldn't have.

Sometimes, if the elder or deacon couldn't reach it to my mom he would actually hand me the dishes and make me pass them to her. The tray of crackers never concerned me much, I was able to receive that tray and pass it on to my mother with little issue. The tray of grape juice was another subject altogether. It was a tray of terror as far as I was concerned. I never once touched that tray without visions of spilling its contents all over the floor, ending the communion service for the day.

Once the communion service was done, the only thing left to look forward to was the invitation/benediction. If I could just make it through that song without anyone getting baptized, I would be a free man.

I was always baffled as to how the elderly man who led singing would always slowly stand up from his seat to the side of the Preacher right as the Preacher was coming to the end of his sermon. He was always ready to step to the pulpit to lead us on the last song.

Hindsight tells me there was probably a hand gesture from the Preacher, which I might have caught had I not been staring at my wristwatch wondering when this service would end. But, at the time, I thought maybe they had worked out a magic word backstage that when the Preacher said it, the elder took his cue to walk forward.

However it was that the song leader knew to make his way to the pulpit, his arrival there meant that all we had to do was sing one last song and we would be done. It was the invitation song, if someone wanted to get baptized and become a Christian they would walk down the aisle as we were singing. The Preacher would whisper something to them as we sang, then as we finished the song the Preacher and soon to be Christian would stand up there and the Preacher would introduce them to the congregation, telling a little about them. He would then ask them to repeat after him and say, "I believe... that Jesus is the Christ... the Son of the Living God" to which the person would repeat.

At this point, there would be a song of celebratory sound and the Preacher and the person to be baptized would walk in the back to prepare for the Baptism. You would hear the Preacher enter the baptismal pool from behind the curtain and you would hear the "to be converted" enter from the other side of the stage. You could hear them wade toward the middle. The curtains would open, the Preacher would be standing there facing the congregation, with the convert looking to the left, backed into the Preacher's arms.

The Preacher would say, "(person's name) because you have professed your love for Jesus Christ, I baptize you in the name of the Father, and of the Son, and of the Holy Spirit". He would dunk the person underwater and as soon as he pulled them up, the piano would play a happy song that everyone would sing and I would know this service was finally about to come to an end.

We had all just witnessed someone giving their life over to Jesus Christ and my primary concern was that this service just got extended by roughly 15 minutes. Hindsight allows me to see the selfishness and the error of my ways, but watching a person be baptized was a pretty painful part of my childhood.

My parents didn't go to church very often, nor did they make me. The church I described above was a non-denominational Christian church, and the only other childhood memory I have from any kind of church was of a Baptist church that was located just up the street from our house.

I have no clue as to why or how I was at that church, perhaps it was a Vacation Bible School week during summer. But whatever reason I was there for, I remember watching a film. The only scene I recall from the film was that of a mother and son in their kitchen with the mother standing over either the sink or the stove. In an instant the mother had disappeared leaving the kid alone in the kitchen. The kid freaked out at his mothers' disappearance, as any child would do.

It was a film about the "Rapture", which I personally find to be ridiculous. As an adult, what I find even more ridiculous, is that any supposedly responsible adult would show that film to a room full of kids. There were other scenarios in the movie, I don't happen to remember any of them other than the scene I just described. It was a shameful act of scare tactics that they used, and legend has it that my father let the Preacher know what he thought of said scare tactics.

I don't know whether it's true or not, or if Pop did confront the Preacher about it, but knowing what I know about Pop back in those days I would put money on the confrontation happening. Doubling down the bet that it was not a very pleasant "chat" to witness at all. We never went back to that church.

My only other memory from that church is that I fell off of a slide when I was five years old and broke my right arm on the playground. I remember falling, standing up and looking at my right arm with a sag in it where it had once been straight and getting a weird feeling in my stomach. I've broken several bones in my right arm, wrist and hand since then and I have always had the same feeling in my stomach.

I have actually hurt my hand before, and because I did not get that feeling in my stomach, assumed that there was no broken bone and went about my day with a sore hand. The Rapture film and the broken arm are the only two memories I have of the Baptist church, but they seemed enough to form a lifetime opinion of what I think of it. It's not my cup of tea. If it is yours, then more power to you, it just wasn't for me.

The only other church I will make mention of is Buffington Road Christian Church, it's the non-denominational Christian church I was dragged to as a child. The only Preacher I will mention period is Lester

Shell, who was the Minister of Buffington Road. Les Shell was a good man.

I am thankful I was not forced to go to church very often as a child, because as I got into high school I chose to willingly attend church. I really got into it for most of my formative years.

I don't think I would have gotten into it as much as I did, or enjoyed it as much as I did, if it were something I was forced to do as a kid. I think I would have just resented it. That doesn't mean that's the case for everyone, but in my case, I think I respond better to something if I happen upon it, not if it's forced down my throat.

Buffington Road had a large youth group, made up of about 90% Cambodian refugees. I never felt like I fit in with anyone from my high school, so this youth group became my only friends, for the most part, throughout high school, though none of them went to my school.

We had a Sunday morning service, a Sunday night service and a Wednesday evening service. The church had a large field and most Sundays we would spend the entire time between morning service and evening service out in that field playing football, soccer or volleyball.

Wednesday evenings there would be a dinner before the service so we would usually get there as early as we could, eat as fast as we could and then go out in the yard and goof around.

That church was pretty much the center of my life for those years, and I can't think of a much better way I could have spent them. I had the time of my life with those friends, I met the girl who would become my wife there, and I met people who would become lifelong friends there.

As I grew older, I became more entrenched in what the bible taught. I read more books about Christianity. I enjoyed telling people what I believed and why I believed it. I liked being able to answer people's questions. I taught youth classes and taught the youth group. I once preached a sermon to the Cambodian elders when my brother, who was the regular Preacher was out of town.

That was over 15 years ago and I still know where the notes to that sermon are. Should I ever find myself at a pulpit being asked to give a sermon, I will reach for those notes and probably give a repeat performance of it. Some of the best memories of my life were made either at that church, or with the people I met there. The building is still there, but it is now some other church. There is a Lester Shell Christian Church not very far from that building but I have never been to it.

Les Shell has been the only person, to date, that could keep me even remotely interested in the sermon. He was funny, he was harsh, he was matter of fact, and he was the epitome of what a Preacher should be.

He was a man I called many times with religious questions and he would always give me an answer that also included the verse he was referring to. This allowed me to look up the verse and see if I agreed with it or not. I think a lot of Preachers just tell you their interpretation of the verse and expect you to take their interpretation as scripture, but not Les Shell. He was cut from a mold that has long since been discontinued.

He married me and Mean Phov, on June 21, 1997. I told him that I wanted only what legally had to be said for us to be married and not much more. I think the elapsed time from when my soon to be wife walked down the aisle, to the time we walked out as newlyweds was about 18 minutes total.

I can't think of one instance where I could say he didn't "practice what he preached." I have never been big on sermons, and I have never been able to flip to a verse and follow along very well.

My mind races too much to concentrate, it always has and it probably always will. But, Les Shell told jokes in sermons well over 20 years ago that I still tell to this day. Here is one joke in particular, which I still tell often, when the time for college football smack talk presents itself to me. Since I am a man who roots for Georgia Tech, I will speak of the time the University of Georgia quarterback was failing out of his math class and was about to be academically ineligible to play football. Being the star quarterback that he was, the UGA alumni made it possible for him to be able to take one math test, to be held in the stadium and open to the public. If he passed the test he would continue to play football and if he failed the test he would be off of the team. Come test day and the stadium is packed, full of UGA alum and current students alike, all there to cheer on their quarterback. The teacher steps up to the microphone and begins the test by asking "What is 2+2?" Perplexed, the quarterback thinks about it for a minute and quietly answers "4?" The stadium jumps to their feet, all in unison and start shouting "GIVE HIM A SECOND CHANCE! GIVE HIM A SECOND CHANCE!"

I would hate to run off any would be readers here just because they happen to like UGA, so I will remind everyone here that it is just a joke. Besides, everyone knows the University of Georgia would never suspend a player for academic reasons (wink wink nudge nudge).

Obviously the joke can be made out for whatever school the teller wishes it to be. I can't remember if Les was a Tech fan or a UGA fan, but I suspect, as most jokes that are told in the Atlanta area, that one of the two schools served as the punch line for that joke.

Every sermon I can remember him giving, and there are many, he always found a way to make you laugh without detracting for the bigger purpose of why you were there to listen to him. Les Shell was a good man.

I've fallen out of the church, though there are many times I miss the life I had when I was active in a church. I think any church I go to, I immediately start comparing the Preacher to Les Shell, which is unfair to anyone, because no one can compete with him.

He didn't need scare tactics to win anyone over, he had Jesus. If you have Jesus and you're trying to sell Jesus, what more do you need? That's enough in and of itself. I quit going to church many years ago, as my Saturday nights usually got in the way of my desire to do much of anything on Sunday morning.

I found that most of my passion with the church had turned into arguing with other religious people. I would search for verses to argue with someone who believed 90% of the same stuff as me, but instead of taking communion every Sunday like me, would take it twice a year. Or, how someone who thought it was perfectly fine to be sprinkled with water instead of fully immersed in water wasn't really baptized.

It was all semantics and it was all just me trying to show that how I interpreted the verse was more correct than how they did, when in reality we should have both been out trying to convert someone who didn't believe it at all. I am no one to voice any opinions on what might or might not happen on Judgment Day, but I don't see "dunked vs sprinkled" being a deal breaker for anyone to enter.

It also seems like churches are comprised of two main groups, those that love the Preacher and those that want him gone. It's my opinion most churches operating nowadays are always powder keg, just waiting to divide and lose half its members.

I hope someday I can find the passion I once had for religion. My life was better when I was active in church. And even though I haven't been in years, I have said prayers here and there.

I have never once, in my life, prayed about something and come out of it feeling worse. That doesn't mean my prayers are always answered, it just means that prayer has always helped comfort me.

I wish I could find that non-denominational Christian church, with Les Shell at the pulpit, telling his jokes and wrapping up his sermon with his secret hidden message to the song leader to get up and head towards him.

I would still most likely lip sync the hymns, but I think I would secretly be hoping that someone would walk down the aisle for during the invitation.

RUNNING DOWN HALLS

Every kid is afraid of certain things that, as an adult, seem pretty ridiculous. While I know this is true, I can't help but think that some of the highlights of my childhood fears are crazy by even the most outlandish standard.

I spent the better part of my childhood running down halls. It seemed as though there was always something evil chasing me. I'm not sure why a hallway represented the most vulnerable place I might find myself, but there were many mad dashes from one end of a hall down to the other end, way too many to count.

First on my list of things that terrified me, we will start with perhaps the most ridiculous. The Wizard of Oz. Not any bad witch scene, not any flying monkeys or even the lollipop guild. No, my fear from the wizard of Oz was the lady riding the bike at the beginning of the movie.

She was to turn into a witch later in the movie, but the scene with her riding a bike with some creepy music in the background scared me to no end. I don't think I walked at a normal, non-panicked pace down the hallway to my house until I was well into my teens.

Every trip down this hallway of terror I envisioned this lady on a bicycle chasing me. Now, my hallway wasn't extraordinarily long. Looking back I would place it no more than 20 feet tops, but to my terrified legs and vivid imagination it may as well have been a 5k course.

I was not yet smart enough to ask myself how she would have gotten herself and her bicycle into the house without anyone's knowledge. Nor was I brave enough to ever turn around and actually confirm that she was indeed both behind me and catching up to me.

Unfortunately for me, as per the design of most any house, the hallway is where I would gain entrance to the living room and kitchen from any of the bedrooms or the bathroom. So it was a path that I had to frequently take.

I say frequently take because being afraid of such trivial things as a lady riding a bike from an old black and white movie tends to wreak havoc on a kids stomach. Now maybe that was not the only thing that caused me to be in the bathroom so much. We were fed a steady diet of meat and potatoes along with all you could eat raw vegetables to snack on.

Whatever the blame, my fear of everything or the endless amounts of roughage that needed to be expelled, I was taking several trips down this dreaded hallway daily.

Another drawback to this particular fear was having to hide it. Being the youngest of four boys, and having a father that would have "given me something to be scared of" meant I had to take this secret fear to the grave. I can only assume Pop would have been happy to give me something to be scared of, as this was his one and only way of dealing with a crying child.

My family is one that shows they love you and care about you by ridiculing anything and everything they can find and hold against you. And I am no pitiful victim in that regard because I give as well as I get, so save the phone call to Dr. Phil, for now anyway.

Having to conceal this fear, this mad dash of panic and terror over the course of a 20 ft. hallway that ended in a living room generally occupied around the clock meant that around 18 to 19 feet I had to come to a screeching halt and wipe the "white girl being chased in the woods of a horror movie" look off of my face. Then attempt to gather my composure and casually saunter into the living room for the last step, convincing whoever may be in there that I had just casually strolled from the back of the house and had in no way both just taken a poo AND cheated death for the third time that day.

I suppose I need to ask my brothers or parents if I was at all successful in keeping them in the dark all these years. Smart money would be on "no" being the answer to that. Looking back I am quite certain that I could not do all that sprinting and not be flushed faced and out of breath even after regaining my composure somewhere after the 18 foot mark.

And since I've never been accused of 'walking on cat's feet' I can probably safely assumed that they all heard me barreling down the hall and just didn't care enough to ask if I had just been involved in a life threatening bicycle chase with a scary looking lady who would someday soon become the representative for all wicked witches coming from the west... or was it east?

Second on my list of unnecessary scars from childhood comes from the few trips to my paternal grandparent's house that we went on as a kid.

I can't remember how many times we went up to see them, it wasn't many. They lived in a northern suburb of Atlanta (Alpharetta) and we lived in a southern suburb (Union City). It wasn't an extremely long ride, I can only assume the reason we didn't go much was because the cars we had back then weren't made for many road trips.

I would say we went up to visit them 20-25 times that I can remember. Not counting the few times we were up there on Christmas Day and were inside the house, anytime we visited them, we always sat on their porch for the duration of the visit. It was a nice porch, screened in with some variation of Astroturf carpeting. It may have had ceiling fans always on. I don't remember ever being horribly uncomfortable on the porch but I do remember always wondering why we weren't inside the house.

Given the length of travel time it would take to get a car which wouldn't go much over 45 mph from the south of Atlanta to the north of Atlanta, and the amount of time my parents would sit on the porch talking to my grandparents about whatever they talked about, there would come a time when I would have to use the bathroom.

And to get to the bathroom I would have to go into the house and down the hallway (see a pattern developing here?). While in that hallway I would be forced to pass the bedroom which was my uncles when he had lived there.

That is where 'it' dwelled. Even thinking back on it now I get a full body shudder. For a reason that has long escaped me, my uncle, when he lived there, had a life size cardboard picture of Elton John leaned over and holding a putter. That cardboard Elton is so burned into my psyche that I could describe it to a police sketch artist and you would know, with one look, that it was Elton John holding a putter.

I don't remember when I realized that it was an inanimate object that could never do me any harm. Keep in mind from the 'lady on a bicycle chasing me' story that I didn't exactly need much in the way of realistic threats to go ahead and assume an attack was imminent.

I'm not even certain I ever stopped to see what it was until years later. I know that my peripheral vision picked up a full grown man, in some kind of menacing pose over in the unused bedroom years ago and in every visit since then, that same full grown man, in that same menacing pose had been lurking in that same bedroom.

How had he not killed my grandparents in their sleep? How does he stay in that room undetected for so many years? Does his back hurt from staying bent over for so long? Why did no one tell me to watch out for the full grown menace man when I got up and said those words I dreaded most at my grandparents' house, "I have to go to the bathroom."

I had waited as long as I could wait. I had to go! I didn't want to go. I would wait to see if someone would go inside the house for something unrelated and I could piggyback their trip inside and sneak a pee.

But as always, no one had to go inside for anything other than me. I can very vividly remember getting inside this house and debating on whether or not to continue to the bathroom. The kitchen was right beside the porch, could I just pee in the kitchen sink and pray no one saw? I never tried, but I did think about it.

The worst part of making it to the bathroom, was speed peeing so I was not in there one second longer than I had to be. I never knew when the bathroom door would open and I would be face to face with Death.

When I say speed pee, imagine if you will, how the mechanics in NASCAR fill up a car with fuel as it hits pit row. A guy runs up to the side of the car with the gas can on his shoulder, there is fuel leaking out of that thing the minute he picks it up. He runs over and puts it in the car and as the car speeds off he runs back to the other side of the wall, with this canister pouring fuel every step of the way.

Ok, now work with me here. Imagine a child, a "ruggedly handsome for his age" kind of child, sprinting down a hallway, making sure that the menacing man was still there in his peripheral vision, unzipping his pants in full gallop, hitting the bathroom door with the hose in open position, peeing as quickly(on purpose) and as inaccurately(on accident) as humanly possible, all while looking over my shoulder for any intruders, leaving the bathroom(maybe a bit too early), zipping up my pants(again, perhaps a bit early) and sprinting back down the hallway.

The pee to toilet ratio was not good at all. The amount of splatter that my poor grandmother must have had to clean after our visits might be why we were not up there much. Maybe we weren't invited, or maybe it took Pop that long to get back on her good side.

All those years I spent petrified and peeing all over everywhere only to find out the menacing man in the room was the same kind fella who brought us "Tiny Dancer." There was a different Rocketman running the halls of that house all those years ago, and he made quite a mess.

On a side note, my grandparents were the only people, to this day, I knew who had a trash compacter. When I wasn't peeing all over bathrooms I spent every spare second at their house looking for stuff I could throw away. My grandmother did always humor me and we would compact something that we could have just as easily crumpled up and thrown away.

The vast majority of what I compacted at her house was probably mini Reese's wrappers but helping clean was the least I could do, since she was going to have a good 10 minute disinfectant job once she checked the bathroom.

Hopefully AFTER we had pointed our car in the southbound direction on I85.

NANNY COOK

I could easily start any chapter I write on my childhood off with the phrase, "It's a shame that youth is wasted on young people." It's one of my favorite quotes, I don't know who said it, but they certainly nailed it with that one.

I think it sums up any phase of my life that could be classified as youth, because I definitely would do a lot of things differently if I could have another run through. I chose to use it for the chapter I would try to write about my maternal grandmother, because that is one of the things, in my lifetime of bad decisions and regrets, in which I really feel that I repeatedly dropped the ball on.

For the remainder of this chapter, this book or anything else you may ever read when I am speaking of my maternal grandmother, she will be referred to as Nanny. Nanny was a constant in my early life, she rented a house across the street from us when I was very young and would watch me during the day while my parents were at work and my brothers were at school.

I don't have many memories of any of that, as it would have all been pre-kindergarten for me. I remember there was always candy in her house and that no one in the history of the earth could make a better cheese toast than her. Five smears of butter strategically placed between the bread and the cheese is mandatory to even hope to contend with her cheese toast.

That goes for cinnamon toast as well, but her cheese toast was the stuff of legends. I think this younger generation, with all the choices of cheeses and fake butters and breads with seeds on the crust, really just doesn't stand a chance. White bread, real butter and sharp cheddar cheese. Anything else is a bastardization of an American classic.

I assume the bulk of my day was spent eating cheese toast and watching TV. I remember her TV sat on a small stand and on the little shelf beneath the TV sat a wind up butterfly cube. I call it a cube, I have no idea what it's called. But you wound it up and two butterflies on metal rods would spin around and it played music.

I was completely entranced with every part of it. The song that it played, Mockingbird, the butterflies that spun around, and the little musical box that sat on the underside that played the music. The music box was a set of pins placed on a revolving cylinder that would spin around and pluck the tuned teeth of a steel comb.

I would stare at that piece the most. Those pins had to be placed perfectly, perfectly spaced apart so as to hit the correct tooth at the exact right time to make the song work. Years later, when Nanny passed, I asked my mother to please get that butterfly music box for me so that I could have it as a reminder of her.

I am pushing 40 years old now, Nanny has been dead for more than 15 years, and that music box still sits on the TV stand in my living room. Once in a while I will grab it and wind the crank, it will play that song from my childhood and take me right back 35 years ago, sitting in my Nanny's living room floor.

I think Nanny talked on the phone a lot while I was there. Or maybe people visited her during the day. I can't remember which. What I know is I would hear her speak often of someone named Eloise (pronounced "Elle-Louise"). I had never met Eloise, I figured she was related to Nanny, either she was her sister or her sister in law or maybe, at most distant, an aunt. What intrigued me most about Eloise was that Nanny always prefaced her name with the word "Poor."

No matter what Nanny was talking about, if she was talking about Eloise, she would say Poor Eloise. If she said the name Eloise a million times, she said "poor" a million times in front of it, "well you remember Poor Eloise went to that doctor" or "Poor Eloise went to Florida that one time." What made this woman so poor? Had I ever met Eloise? Would I ever meet Eloise? Would I know right away what made her so poor or would I be left wondering? I needed to know about Poor Eloise.

I never thought to ask Nanny when she got off the phone or when her visitors had left what had gone wrong in Eloise's life for her to be forever called Poor Eloise. Perhaps she distracted me with candy or cheese toast, but for whatever reason, I never thought to ask her.

Sometime well into my 30's I remembered Poor Eloise, probably drinking whiskey and staring at my Nanny's old music box had stirred the memory. I had gone my whole life without meeting Eloise and now I needed answers.

I called my mother for a quick lesson on the family tree and was met by confusion. She kept telling me she didn't know anyone in our family named Eloise. There are many things I can't remember, like what I had for lunch yesterday, or where I am supposed to be tomorrow, but I know that I remembered Nanny saying Poor Eloise many a day during my childhood.

When I used the preceding qualifier "poor" to remind my mother of Eloise it was then that she knew who I was talking about. Louise, her aunt and my Nanny's sister. It seems that my entire childhood curiosity about this poor family member of mine was based on me not understanding my grandmother's pronunciation.

Poor Eloise was actually "poor ole Louise," my Nanny's sister. And the catastrophic life event that deemed her as forever poor was that she had married a bum of a man. Poor ole Louis and her bum husband. I never met either one of them. I assume they had both died before I was born.

My maternal grandfather, Nanny's husband, had also died before I was born. He died in 1975, I was born in March of '76. Pawpaw Cook is what they called him. His name was Jeff Cook. Nanny and her brother and sisters, along with my aunts would often call me the "spitten image" of Jeff Cook.

I had obviously never met the man, but apparently not only did I look just like him, I also had his quick temper. It was nice to feel a connection to someone I had never met, and it was nice to have the attention of great aunts when you see them once or twice a year. They spoke very fondly of him, and since I was a reminder of him it made me feel good about myself. I would look forward to them calling me Jeff Cook, which I would usually get called a few times whenever I was in their presence.

To add an interesting side note to this story, a few years ago while drinking with a Buddhist pal of mine, I was telling him how I was always called my grandfather's name by those who knew him and he told me that, along with the fact that I was born less than a year after he died, meant that I was him reincarnated.

I don't know if it was the alcohol talking, or maybe he was just pulling my leg. He may have really believed it to be a strong possibility. I don't think I would have disappointed my mother as many times as I have, or have as many regrets as I have about how I treated Nanny if I had been Jeff Cook incarnate.

Nanny moved a little further away shortly after I started school. She was still pretty close by, but moved to some apartments, I remember her more there than at the house across the street.

I think the apartments were some kind of government assisted living, but am not sure. The section she was in was predominately elderly people. It was several buildings in a U shaped design with a pool and a clubhouse in the middle. We swam in the pool a few times and held her a few birthday parties in the clubhouse, but other than that we never had anything to do with anything but her tiny apartment.

You walked into a small living room, which led to a small kitchen, which led to a bedroom that was just large enough to hold a bed. I remember how impressed I was with her street smarts one day when I learned that her phone number in the phone book was listed under Jeff Cook still, many years after his death.

She never had it changed out of fear that some ne'er do well may be perusing the phone book and find a female name listed and think they had an easy target. That was, I guess my first introduction in the "trust no one" mentality that I have carried with me throughout my life.

She was the first, and only person I've ever heard be described as a "yellow dog democrat". When I asked what that meant I was told that, "she would vote for a yellow dog before she voted for a republican". It made sense to me (the explanation, not how anyone could ever vote for a democrat, human or canine) so I never pursued it any further than that explanation.

I know my grandmother thought it was absolutely unforgivable to have a pecan laying on the ground not picked up. The house we grew up in had a pecan tree in the front yard and a pecan tree in the back yard, each fully grown and fully fruiting.

Those trees dropping their pecans, along with Nanny's obsession with collecting every one of them, meant that I spent a lot of time in the fall picking up pecans. It was a chore that I hated to do. I have never been good at hiding my emotions, so I am sure I made quite the sour face when Nanny would ask me to go collect the fallen pecans.

I always did it, because you didn't say no to your grandmother. I can't vouch for how well I covered the ground in search of them, but I did usually come back with a pretty good haul which she would keep on her table and we would keep on ours.

I wish I could go back and search a yard for pecans for her. I hope to one day have a yard with some mature pecan trees. I am embarrassed to look back and think how sour my face and/or body language must have been when she would ask me to do something so simple as to pick up pecans for her. It's a shame that youth is wasted on young people.

Nanny never learned to drive a car. I'm not sure if she ever worked a job in her life, but she didn't work a job in my lifetime. She had three daughters, all of whom lived relatively close, but we were the closest to her so a lot of routine daily trips fell to my mom or my brothers as they became old enough to drive.

I doubt very seriously that her daily planner was ever filled with too much. A few trips to the doctor and the grocery store per month was probably the extent of her travel needs. As I turned 16 and got a car some of the trips were passed on to me.

It was probably more like 18 before I was ever really asked to do anything, because I can't think of a scenario before then that my mother wouldn't have been able to take Nanny wherever she needed to go.

Once I was out of school then it may have been me who was the only one available during the day to take her somewhere. Let me be clear here when describing my taxi duties for my grandmother, at most, at absolute most, we are talking about a trip to the grocery store once in a blue moon and a trip to her doctor which was 3 minutes down the road once in a blue moon. That is at most.

Yet somehow, in my self-obsessed brain, I can remember thinking that it was as if they had asked me to drive her non-stop from Atlanta to Houston and back. I mean, I had stuff to do, important stuff, why couldn't my mom take off work or call out sick so she could run her mom 30 minutes south.

In keeping with my complete lack of ability to hide my emotions, I am sure I was a complete asshole the entire time I was chauffeuring her around town. I am, at least, confident in saying I was never blatantly disrespectful but I would bet I was less than pleasant.

When I look back at all the time I had to ask her questions, to enjoy her company, I really feel like I missed a golden opportunity. I should have jumped at the chance to be able to spend some time with her. To make it all the worse, I already knew what it was like to not have a grandfather, as she had been widowed before I was born, and here I was taking my grandmother for granted.

The version of me that sits and writes this would enjoy just one ride with his Nanny to her doctor in Palmetto, Georgia. I would drive as slow as possible and ask as many questions as I could think of and get to know her as well as I could.

I would be horrified if my kids felt that my mother was an inconvenience to them the way I did my grandmother. Of course, my children are not as selfish as their father is, so I doubt very seriously that I, or my mother has to worry. It's a shame that youth is wasted on young people.

I guess the one thing that I can never get over, or forgive myself for, is how I acted in her final days. I don't remember the details, presumably because I was too wrapped up in myself to pay attention or care, but I know she went in for an exploratory surgery to see what was going on with something ailing her.

I don't know what was ailing her, or what they were exploring for but I really didn't think anything of it. She had been through a few minor procedures before and had come out stronger than ever.

She was ridiculously active, taking several trips a year up to Washington D.C. and anywhere else her family would take her. Her family that didn't treat her as an inconvenience, I should say.

There was nothing anywhere in her history that would have led any of us to believe that this exploratory surgery would have been anything other than a run of the mill procedure. It was such an afterthought of an operation that my one brother in Washington D.C., who spoiled Nanny the likes of which no grandson has ever spoiled their grandmother before or since, asked her before she went in if she wanted him to fly down before her surgery or after. She told him to just come down after so she would be feeling better for his visit.

Well, needless to say, something went wrong in the "run of the mill" exploratory surgery and Nanny never made it out of the hospital. Without asking someone with a better memory for help, and I don't think I will for the purposes of this writing, I can't remember how long she lasted from the day of her surgery until she died.

I do remember there was a few times that the hospital would call the house and tell us that if we wanted to see her alive again that we needed to get up to the hospital quickly. The fact that they made that call, and we made that run more than once speaks volumes to the strength of my grandmother.

The problem with Nanny's toughness as it pertained to me, is that I didn't inherit any of it. Though I may have ridden up to the hospital with the family, I never brought myself to go into her room and visit her.

In the beginning of it all I could justify my selfishness by telling myself that I "didn't want to see her like that" and that worked for me. It never dawned on me that maybe SHE would want to see ME.

It was nothing more than fear that stopped me from visiting with her. The older I get, with children now and envisioning that they might one day have children, the thought of me laying on my deathbed and knowing that someone I loved was sitting on the other side of the door, too chicken shit to come in and hold my hand and look me in the eye so I could see them, and touch them, rips me up inside.

It is the epitome of selfishness and cowardice I displayed in front of my entire family. Anytime the subject of Nanny comes up, I am filled with shame and regret, and I can feel all eyes falling on me, remembering how I acted.

I remember in either second or third grade, my school did an "adopt a grandparent' program with us. We would send letters and pictures to residents of a retirement home. We each had one adopted grandparent assigned to us, so all of our stuff went to them and anything they sent back to us, we would get.

We planned a field trip to go spend the day with our "grandparents". We would have lunch with them and everything else you do at a retirement home, which must not be much, because I don't remember much in the way of activities that day.

What I remember is spending most of the day in near hyperventilation state, crying from seeing my "grandmother." There were several of the elderly outside waiting on us, but mine was not. So, they took me to her room and I walked in on a lady lying on a bed, hooked up to machines who may or may not have even been conscience.

I have no clue how they expected me to react, I like to think that had they known I was going to freak out and be inconsolable for the rest of the day they may have just lied to me and said my "grandparent" had checked herself out for the day.

I think it would have been easier to take that she deserted me than to walk in on her in some odd state of being not quite alive but not yet dead. Needless to say, I did not spend any time with her that day, outside of that initial meeting, and I bolted on her.

I guess I was as much comfort to my dying adopted grandmother as I would be many years later to my real grandmother.

I remember where I was at when I got the news Nanny had died. I was at my girlfriend's house. She would later become my wife, but I think at that time we were not yet married. We were at her house in College Park, right down the street from the hospital Nanny died in.

There was some kind of party, or celebration going on. I remember hanging up their phone, telling someone that my grandmother had just died and going and sitting in a chair alongside the wall and being numb.

I was one of very few English speakers in the room, so I sat there trying to keep a blank stare on my face. I could hear them talking, and I knew they were talking about me, although I had no idea what they were saying. What I knew was that I knew they were all watching me, seeing how I was handling this news I had just received.

I knew that I had to show no emotion on my face, for in my mind, any emotion shown would only be perceived as weakness. One of my brothers had told me a few years earlier, as we were going into one of my paternal grandparents funeral that if I felt like I was going to cry to think about something else.

At that time in my life I was wrestling for my High School, so that was what I thought about, practices, matches or both. I stared ahead as if I was listening intently, but my mind was replaying wrestling matches. To this day I refer back to this practice, still using matches that I wrestled in 20 years ago.

So that was how I handled the news that day that Nanny had died. Sitting with my back against the wall, listening to people speak a language I didn't understand, thinking intently about a wrestling match that I probably lost, so I wouldn't remind myself that I just let my grandmother die without even saying goodbye to her.

FATHER OF MINE

My father, as of the time of this writing, has been a 38 year study in the combination of brilliance mixed with insanity. My mother believed in the tried and true "wait until your father gets home" form of punishment. Most of my childhood was spent hoping Pop would run away with a new family or be involved in a fiery auto crash on the way home. In hindsight, of course, I am glad neither of these scenarios ever unfolded but I would be lying if I said younger Toby wouldn't have done some pretty bad things to his Daddy voodoo doll.

Being the youngest child of 4 boys, with 6 years between me and the second youngest, I will say that my spankings were minimal compared to the ones they got. Of course, I should also say I was probably a much better kid than those other three. I only remember two or maybe three spankings and I think they were all report card related.

Frankly, I deserved many more than I got. In fact, if I try hard enough I can probably blame all of my adult problems on my parents for not spanking me enough. What a wonderful generation I belong to.

Pop never asked much out of me and I never delivered much. He wanted good grades, Georgia Tech and maybe for one of his kids to work for the railroads. Not wanting to spoil him and only have him expect more out of me, I personally chose to give him none of the above.

Though I do consider myself one of the smartest people I know, high school Toby figured a C without trying was just as good as an A that might require a little effort. All he ever wanted was for me to have it easier than he had it.

I can see that now that I am a father, a father who struggles to pay the house note month to month. But to me back then, he was a just a big mean guy trying to run my life. I couldn't have that. I'm an Aries!

I never appreciated how funny he was when I was younger. He had lines for everyone and every occasion. He never met a stranger, I know that. That used to bug me to no end. I hate talking to people I don't know. I don't even want to watch a conversation being had between someone I know and someone I don't know. It makes me uncomfortable and to that, there was never a shortage of me feeling uncomfortable around my father.

A lady in the Walmart parking lot approaches selling peanut brittle? Pop's response: "I have false teeth, that stuff is Peanut Brutal!" He would overemphasize the word brutal, and they would both laugh while I would cringe on the outside and die a little on the inside.

Then there was the line he said to every teacher of mine he ever met at "Back to School" registration. The day you go meet your teacher for the year. He had but one line, and he used it on every teacher he ever met of mine. "I had him all summer and didn't call you once" was his introduction to my new teacher. My response would be the all too typical outward cringe/inward die that I usually experienced around him and strangers.

The teacher would usually laugh nervously, unsure if he was being serious or not. I can appreciate how funny that line is now that I am old myself. What's even funnier is now that he has grandkids, he will come down to meet them every school year and still say the exact line to them. Every teacher, every year.

I think the teachers still respond with the nervous laughter that they always have, but the difference is this time around instead of cringing and dying on the inside I am delighted that he is saying it, and that my kids have him around to make them cringe in public.

I once got in trouble in middle school. For all the stupid things I've done in my life, I don't remember ever getting in too much trouble, until 8th grade. My introduction into school yard crime and punishment was getting caught buying a pack of "Now or Laters" from a kid at school.

That's not drug lingo for any synthetic pill. I am talking about the actual candy called "Now or Laters." They were big back when I was middle school and I bought a pack from the kid who sold candy at school. Hardly a very heinous act by today's standards, with what kids are buying and selling in schools now, but back then it was a crime that was punished with a few days in ISS (In School Suspension).

The Assistant Principal sent a letter home to my parents informing them that I would be spending the next few days in the ISS room. This was probably a fairly stock letter that he sent out several times a day, but he had never sent one to my father.

He had also never proofread it apparently. My father, took it upon himself to go over this letter with a red ink pen, much the same way a college literary teacher might go over a freshman's essay paper. That letter had so much red ink scribbled on it by the time Pop was done with it you would have thought he was an editor for the Atlanta Journal.

He had put commas where commas should have been, completely reworded some sentences, added a period here and there, and if I am not mistaken I think he added a personal note to the top of it that said something to the effect of "One would think a middle school Assistant Principal would do a better job at composing a letter."

I'm positive that I put it much more nicely than it would have appeared on that letter in red ink, lo those many years ago. But, as I looked at what my father had done to that letter, a few things began to dawn on me about the old man.

Primarily, he was insane. The rumors had been true. The story about him confronting the Baptist Preacher over the Rapture film was true. The story about him getting out of our car and going back and yelling at some guy to "get off his ass he had kids in the car" had to be true as well.

What I also saw in him, was someone who had my back. Now don't get me wrong about Pop, he was not one of those parents who would back their kid up if their kid was wrong. He was actually the opposite, especially when it came to school. Generally speaking, the teacher was always right, as well it should be.

But to lose 3 days of instruction time over a pack of "Now or Laters" was not something he was going to accept. I liked it. I loved it. Right up until he handed the letter back to me and told me to take that to the Assistant Principal first thing in the morning and put it on his desk.

Up to this point, I had (wrongly) assumed that Pop would be delivering this letter to the A.P. This letter that had more red on it than the most harshly graded book reports I had ever seen. Now, the onus was on me to get this "revised" letter returned to its sender, I got a little nervous.

Nonetheless, I went into his office the next day, mumbled "my dad said to give this to you" as quickly and unintelligibly as possible, threw it in the direction of his desk, and high-tailed it out of his office, trying to get as far away as possible before he had a chance to read it.

He did read it, and it ended with me and my father having to meet with the Principal the next day before school began. This is probably a good time to reiterate that this was all over a 25 cent pack of candy.

The next morning, Pop and I arrive and we sit outside the office until the principal calls us in. It wasn't a long wait, and the principal, while I had never had any dealing with him never seemed like a bad guy.

He was a big tall man, intimidating in stature, but there were no stories of him beating up kids floating around the school. Pop and I are called into the office, Pop walks in and lays a tape recorder on this big tall man's desk. It's the old school tape recorders, much like the ones our middle school media center would have been littered with. Pop sets the tape recorder down on his desk, says something like "Everything we talk about today will be recorded and it will go to my lawyer."

He then hits record and play at the same time (for anyone under 30 reading this that's how you did it back then). Because of my poor memory, I don't remember how their conversation went that day. I spent the remainder of the meeting wondering just who the hell our family lawyer was and why I had never met him.

I never would find out who our lawyer was, nor would I ever meet him. But I also never met the inside of the In School Suspension room either. I learned that day that if you are going to bluff, bluff hard. And if you're going to play the crazy card, play it to the end, and most importantly, play it in bright red ink. There were no more notes ever sent to the Nix home from Camp Creek Middle School.

There are lines that if you spent any time around him, you would hear him say over and over. If you ever wanted to borrow anything from anyone he would remind you "don't... touch... other... folks... stuff." He would put a slight pause between every word and even though I have not heard it said in over twenty years, I can still recite it perfectly in his cadence. Apparently, in his head, there was never an instance where borrowing anything turned out well, so he chose to never endorse any form of it.

"Well I don't like it but I'm not going to say anything about it" was another saying he was fond of using any chance he could. If you went to him with an idea or a plan, or needing any advice, you usually didn't get much else other than "Well, I don't like it, but I'm not going to say anything about it". That was his way of telling you that whatever you were planning to do was not a good idea.

The fact that he said he didn't like it, while saying he wasn't going to say anything about it, was just another example of his wit. Which I happen to think is brilliant, the older I get.

Pop smoked cigarettes most of his life. I don't know what age he started, but I know he smoked throughout my childhood. He smoked menthols. To be exact, he smoked "Benson and Hedges Deluxe Menthol 100s". I know this for two reasons. One is because I grew up in a generation where a dad could send his son into a gas station to buy him cigarettes before the son was old enough to reach the counter. It was always an honor for me to go in and buy him cigarettes while he waited in the car because it made me feel grown.

In addition to making me feel grown, it was also a nice early introduction into panic attacks. "Benson and Hedges Deluxe Menthol 100s" is a lot for a small brain to remember. I would repeat it all the way from the car to the counter, and hope that I had the right pack in my hand when I made it back to the car.

The second reason I remember his brand is that it was the first kind of cigarettes I smoked. I smoked them because I stole them from him, to do so. In the beginning I didn't even know how to inhale, so I just sat out behind the house, along with my childhood chums, Nick and Brad, and we would pretend to smoke cigarettes.

I think Brad was really smoking them at that time, and he may have actually already had a 2 pack a day habit by the ripe old age of nine, but Nick and I were doing well to just successfully light one up.

I did eventually learn how to smoke and it was a habit that had for almost twenty years. To say it was a habit takes away from what it really was, an addiction... an addiction that I loved. Quitting smoking was by far the hardest thing I have had to quit so far, and not a day goes by that I don't think about eating a pack of menthol cigarettes.

I miss smoking the most over my morning coffee. Nanny Cook said when she quit smoking that coffee never tasted as good to her, and she was right. Pop quit smoking when his doctor told him that there was absolutely nothing else he could do for him if he continued to smoke.

He had already had a quadruple bypass surgery years before, when I was still in high school. I remember that when they brought him home he was withdrawing from the nicotine. I remember he had the wildest look in his eyes that night that I have ever seen a human being have in their eyes. They brought Pop home from the hospital, and though he had no more available veins for them to use should he ever need another surgery, he wanted a cigarette.

My mother, seeing the same crazy eyes that I was seeing, decided that if anyone was going to survive that night, she was going to have to get him cigarettes. In a decision that baffles me to this day, my mother and my brother left me alone with "ole crazy eyes" to go buy him some smokes.

It was only a 10 minute ride back and forth to the gas station, but it felt like they were gone hours to me. I assume it felt like they were gone for days to him. I was pretty sure they would find my dead body still smoldering from whichever end he had tried to light me from, in hopes that I had some left over nicotine coursing through my veins that he may be able to get a fix from.

In the end, they made it home with his cigarettes, and we all slept with one eye open. He may have actually slept with both crazy eyes open, I'm not sure he was capable of blinking that night.

Reba Mcintyre did a song called "The greatest man I never knew" and that song always stuck out to me and makes me think of my father. He is still alive and well, but it makes me sad for some reason. I don't remember all the words of the song at the moment. I do know that in all my life I've never been able to figure him out. If I ever needed anything, and he had the means, whatever I needed would very quickly become mine.

I also remember the time I announced to my family that I would be getting a divorce. Pop came down to my wife's and my house at the time to give us a speech. It was during this speech that I realized not only would my father lay down his life for his family, but through the screaming and crying and spitting he might very well do so right then, in that moment, in the living room of my soon to be broken home.

I sat there in shock, not knowing if I was about to be fighting or rendering CPR, as he threatened to take the kids from us if we couldn't work it out. I didn't have the heart to tell him just then that the courts usually required more than a philandering father to award custody to grandparents.

All I could think, through all this, was how upset my three brothers were going to be with me when I told them Pop had dropped dead in my living room begging me not to leave my family. Would I still be invited to family gatherings? Would my nephews forever call me "Grandpa Killer" when they happened upon a photo of me that had not been burned at the effigy party?

Luckily for me, Pop survived that morning at my house. The divorce did go through, if only for a year or two. And no, I was not invited to any family functions for quite some time.

As of this writing, I think the only person who hasn't forgiven me for that phase of my life is me.

A lot of daddy songs make me sad. I am not sure why. I can't say that my father was a bad guy, he had his problems, but everyone does. He raised 4 boys on a pretty low income. Conway Twitty singing "That's my job" has always made me sad, even as a kid.

"Daddy's hands" and "The Walk" are two more that always get a reaction out of me. They make me worry and they make me sad. I wish I had appreciated how smart, funny and witty he has always been.

I wasted a lot of years thinking he didn't know what he was talking about or being embarrassed by the things he would say. The very things I now find funny. I don't like watching the man I feared most of my life grow older, becoming more fragile and less intimidating.

Now that I'm a father, I can hear these songs from the other point of view. What songs will my children think of when they look back at me? Will they think happy thoughts or sad thought? I just hope "Cats in the cradle" never triggers a memory.

The Finish line is approaching

As of this writing, my wife is about to begin her trek back to the occidental side of the world. She will fly from Cambodia to Kuala Lumpur, then to Tokyo, Los Angeles, Houston before arriving home in Atlanta.

I have played Mr. Mom for just over three weeks. I have managed this three weeks a lot like I managed 5K's when I would run them. The emphasis being on any word other than "run."

Week one: just like the start of a 5K, I came out of the gate running. I was cooking breakfast and dinner. I was cleaning. I had a good handle on the dishes.

I even threw away all the old Chobani yogurt containers my wife keeps as Tupperware. Trying to get something out of the cabinet she keeps those in is like playing a kitchen version of Jenga.

I was feeling pretty good about myself. I figured this was going to be a breeze. I'm much more domesticated than I ever gave myself credit for.

Week two was a lot like mile two. I was coming to the realization that I had not properly paced myself during mile one... or week one. I was too far away from the starting line to go back, yet I was still much further away from the finish line than I wished I was.

Maybe I should just lay down in the middle of the course and wait for one of the volunteers to bring a golf cart to get me to the finish line. There was a pile of clean, but unfolded, clothes in the laundry room large enough to carve the likeness of three mounted confederate soldiers if one so chose.

I am not nearly as domesticated as I thought I was. I have all the homemaking skills of a Neanderthal.

Week three was keeping right in line with mile three of a 5K. I was pretty certain the finish line was somewhere up ahead, but equally certain I would never live to see it.

I figured if there were no clean dishes available there was no way we could dirty any new ones. That seemed like pretty sound logic, but I think the dirty dish pile was still growing.

The two week supply of paper plates and sandwich making food had lasted us about three days. The kids were beginning to look at me the same way Wile E. Coyote would look at the Roadrunner when he was imagining a giant turkey leg. They offered to draw me a hot bath one night but I declined when I saw them holding carrots behind their backs.

This entire three weeks can be summed up in the following story, sad as it is but true.

I went to the grocery store yesterday to get a loaf of rye bread. Nothing more, nothing less. I spent over $100.00 and realized once I got home that I still didn't have any rye bread.

My wife will be home in the next couple of days. And much like the finish line of a 5K where I strut around, flexing, like I could have had a better finishing time if I had wanted, I will pretend as if I had a full grasp on the situation at home the entire time.

I just hope she doesn't read this column.

Georgia Sports Fan

I wish I could enjoy sports but I'm from Georgia.

I don't think we pick our sports teams, I believe we are assigned our teams from birth. I was born in Atlanta and raised in Union City. That gives me the Atlanta Braves, Falcons and Hawks, along with the Georgia Tech Yellow Jackets. For badder or for worse.

I grow to love the 1995 Atlanta Braves more and more each year. I wonder if they take a celebratory toast each year another state team fails to win a championship, like the '72 Dolphins take when the last unbeaten team loses a game each year in the NFL.

At this point, the '95 Braves are the only thing saving us, the state of Georgia, from being the subject of our very own "30 for 30." A special titled something like "Choking on the Chattahoochee."

The older I get, the less I find myself able to sit through any sport. And that is coming from a guy who used to keep ESPN on all day, even though it usually repeated itself hour after hour.

Of course, back when I watched ESPN was when they broadcast sports and not liberal politics. Maybe that has something to do with my waning interest in sports, too.

Eric Gregg and his 1997 strike zone for Livan Hernandez pretty much killed the sport of baseball for me. I don't know that I have watched a full game since that day.

Growing up during what I believe was the greatest era of NBA basketball made me washing my hands of that sport particularly painful. I grew up with Magic vs. Bird, the Detroit Bad Boys, Michael Jordan and the Human Highlight reel.

I should have given up on the NBA when 'Nique was robbed in Chicago in 1988 but I held on. It was in 2007 when Robert Horry hip-checked Steve Nash and the announcers acted as if he had stabbed him that I saw the end of my love for the NBA approaching.

Fast forward to 2012 when the Spurs were fined for resting their starters before the playoffs. The league literally said they did a disservice to the league and their fans. By resting their star players before the playoffs began.

That was it for me. A head coach's entire life should revolve around doing whatever puts his team in the best position to win a championship. To punish him for doing so, because resting his players affected television ratings and upset the ticket buying public moved the NBA from a sport to entertainment, for me.

I don't have enough space in this, or any column I write, to list how ridiculous football has become. From tuck rules to not knowing what constitutes a catch anymore. Ronnie Lott would have aggravated assault warrants taken out for him if he hit someone today like he spent his entire career hitting people.

I know this is one of those that will land me in the "grumpy old man" category. But I'm okay with being a grumpy old man. I wear it well.

At least Vince McMahon quit insulting our intelligence and quit pretending like he was presenting an actual sporting event and called it what it was – sports entertainment. Perhaps it's time some other sports do the same.

Law Enforcement Habits

Recently I had a friend ask me what I told my family about my job.

For those of you not in the know, I work in law enforcement. Other than typically trying to downplay most things I see or do, I had never given it much thought. I know they worry, so I try to alleviate as much of that as one can do in this profession.

The way social media is these days, it is possible they may hear about particularly bad scenes while I am still on them. That's just the nature of the beast. I don't lie to them about what happened, but I do leave out any details I don't want them to hear.

I don't lie to them about the world we live in. I try to keep them in a protected bubble as much as I can, but I let them know there are bad people out there. Not misunderstood people. Not people who didn't get enough hugs as a kid and like to act out. Just straight up bad people who do straight up bad things for no reason.

Dr. Phil and the judicial system can figure out how to fix them. I just want my kids to know they exist, and how to deal with them should they ever be forced to.

They know when we are eating out that I will sit facing the door. I don't like anyone behind me. That's not a habit I picked up when I started this career, but it is definitely one I am not giving up anytime soon.

Hypervigilance is an enhanced state of sensory sensitivity accompanied by an exaggerated intensity of behaviors whose purpose is to detect activity. In other words, viewing everyone you ever meet as a potential threat. I guess it goes without saying, at this point, that I don't care much for large crowds.

Because I work in the same area I live, I will often see people I have dealt with on the job while I am out with my family. Depending on what the basis of our work-related encounter was, some people may not like me as much as I would prefer they did.

My children know if we are ever in public and I reach for my weapon to get as far away from me as they can, as quickly as possible.

One of the more interesting habits I have formed since I began this career is I very rarely carry anything in my right hand anymore. That's my dominant hand, the one closest to my weapon.

I don't remember how I developed this habit, but I have found myself subconsciously carrying things in my left hand even on off days around the house. I find it fascinating that my body has learned a complete new way of doing something in just a few years, after a lifetime of doing the opposite.

I don't like going to either of my children's schools in uniform because I don't want them to catch any grief from classmates who have been brought up to not like/trust/respect a person in uniform.

I don't put blue line stickers on our personal vehicles. Not because I am not proud of what I do for a living. Outside of my family, I have never been more proud of anything in my life than I am of my current job.

I just don't want to put my family in possible harm's way from someone who may wish to harm those in this profession.

Running in a 5K

I ran a 5K last weekend.

If my math is correct that is one K for every degree it was that morning. I don't usually recommend running in such cold weather but it was for the Angel's House, which is a cause worth braving the harsh weather for.

My body was not designed for running, so no matter how cold it may be, I will sweat. Because of this, I wore shorts and a T-shirt. That decision, while made in my heated house that morning, was quickly regretted while standing outside at the starting line.

Speaking of the starting line, every 5K I ever run I always feel like when the person in charge is giving the runner's directions before the start, they always look directly at me when they give the "slower runners keep right" reminder.

I started out of the gate at a good pace, for me. Within the first half mile or so, some kids got in front of me. They weren't bothering me or in my way because, quite frankly, I couldn't have passed them if I had wanted to.

These kids looked to be maybe six years old, and they were leaving me in the dust. When I was six I could run the distance from home plate to first base in kickball. That's about it. I usually didn't have to run much more than that because most of the time we had to use "ghost men" on most of the bases. The funny thing about these kids is they weren't even using their arms to run.

A 5K to them did not require full body effort. They even started running in a zig zag pattern at one point as if they were running away from an alligator. I guess 3.1 miles was not enough for them, they needed to add a degree of difficulty to the course.

As if that were not bad enough, somewhere between miles one and two a guy pushing a stroller passed me. It was a pretty big stroller too, so this guy was effectively lifting weights while running. Not only that, I think he was feeding the kid in the stroller, because there was a half-eaten banana and a sippy cup up near the handle.

It was taking all I had to keep my earplugs lodged in my ears as I plodded along, and this guy was multitasking his way down Spence Avenue. I couldn't see what was on his phone, but he was probably doing his doing his taxes.

My ego was already taking a pretty decent beating that morning. I have never confused myself with being a runner, but I like to think I'm in decent shape.

Then a lady wearing jeans passed me. She may have even been wearing high heels, I don't know. The joke is on her though, I'm not even sure jeans and high heels are in style this time of year.

I couldn't look down to confirm the high heels. By that point of the race, my tears had left my face pretty well frozen. Without going into details, I am fairly certain I looked like the moped scene from "Dumb and Dumber."

In all seriousness, it was a great time and for a great cause. When you see "Angel's Run 5K" come up on the calendar next year, please consider running it. I can pretty much guarantee you, no matter what your fitness level, that if I am there you will not come in last place.

Women – the weaker sex?

I don't know who ever came up with the bright idea to refer to women as the "weaker sex."

I do know, with certainty, it was not anyone who has ever spent any time in a protective suit helping teach a ladies' self-defense class.

Maybe calling them the weaker sex makes us fellas feel better about not getting out of bed all weekend when we catch a common cold, otherwise known as a man-flu. I'm not sure. I don't care what we call them, I know I am going to continue to milk a low-grade fever for as long as I possibly can.

I can be certain of this inaccurate nickname women have been given because I have spent time in a protective suit, helping teach a ladies' self-defense class.

The agency I work for offers a ladies' self-defense class several times a year. It's a 3-4 hour course that includes a couple of hours in the classroom, culminating in a chance for the participants to put what they have just learned into practice.

We have a sucker, I mean volunteer – which, for the purposes of this story is me – don a full body protective suit and "attack" the ladies, one at a time. The ladies, in turn, get their chance to take everything they have just learned and beat the tar out of the sucker... I mean volunteer.

Now I am no martial arts master by any stretch.

I wrestled in high school. I have trained with professional mixed martial artists, both in boxing and Brazilian jiu jitsu. And as is the norm in my profession, I am trained in various hand-to-hand combat situations throughout the given year.

Until I volunteered to help with this class, all of my experience in any type of training had been with other guys. So it is here that I will dispute the "fairer sex" nickname is as inaccurate as the "weaker sex" moniker.

In my experience, if you are wearing protective headgear and the person you are grappling with rips that headgear off your head while they are delivering knee strikes to your face, they are usually going to stop, let you reset your helmet and then continue with the beat down they were giving you.

That seems "fair" to me. But that was not the case in this particular ladies' self-defense class. Not only did this lady not stop pulling the helmet off my head, but I think she started kneeing me faster.

It was like the scene in "A Christmas Story" when Ralphie is beating up the bully, except this lady wasn't crying. I think she was laughing. I couldn't actually hear her laughing because, by this point, my ears had become handles she could use to help get my face to her knee faster. Which is exactly what she had just been taught.

Based on my experience as a "volunteer" for this ladies' self-defense class, I can assure you ladies are not the weaker sex. And I can argue with you that they are not the fairer sex.

The next time you see a lady out in public and think you want to bother her, ask yourself how certain you can be that she hasn't taken one of our self-defense classes. Trust me, your ears are better used for hearing than they are for handles.

As for me, I think I caught a sniffle typing this column. I better go lay back in bed and whine until I get some chicken noodle soup.

*Please feel free to contact my agency to sign up for the next ladies' self-defense class. Unless you're still mad at me for the time I wrote about loud mufflers.

No Particular Pier

I liked being a father much more when my son's toughest decision was which "Wiggle" was the best.

He just took off walking toward the pier closest to our condo. He left me sitting here in a beach chair, overlooking the Gulf of Mexico. This is my happy place.

It seems like just yesterday I dropped him off for his first day at daycare and made a conscious effort to not look back. I didn't look back because I was afraid if we made eye contact he would start crying and I would have to turn around and pick him back up.

Truth be told, if we had made eye contact after I dropped him off, one of us would have most certainly cried, though I am not certain which one of us it would have been.

Now every few minutes I take my gaze off the ocean to look over to see if I can still see him walking toward the pier. I like having him – and his little sister – in my line of sight. I wish I could always have my eyes on them, but that's not how life works.

He is officially out of sight now, but I can see the pier. I know that's his destination.

We are at a point in our lives, in this country, where we can't even take our kids to school without worrying about their safety.

My son told me last week he was thinking about joining the Marines after he graduated high school. If that's what he wants, then I am fine with that decision. I just want him to be happy.

I used to want him to be successful, but success means different things to different people. His definition of success may not be the same as mine.

But we both know what happiness is. That's what I want for him.

I went for a walk this morning myself. I walked past a man sitting on the beach holding a baby in his lap, presumably that baby's first trip to the beach.

I got a good look at him as I got closer and I saw myself. Yesterday I was sitting on this very same beach, holding my son in my lap on his first trip down.

Then I looked a little closer and I saw the day before yesterday. I was the baby, with my father holding me in his lap on my first trip down.

I wanted to grab that man by the shoulders and tell him to do everything in his power to not blink. He is going to blink and when he opens his eyes that baby boy is going to be telling him what his plans are for after high school.

But he wouldn't believe me. Not today. Today I am just an old man watching his son walk off toward a pier.

He will believe me tomorrow though. Tomorrow it will be him looking up from the ocean to see if he can still see his son off in the distance, as he makes his way down to whatever pier they happen to be staying near.

I can't blame him. I wouldn't have believed an old man on the beach yesterday, either.

I have walked to my fair share of piers in my life. More than a few of them I had no business walking to. In the back of my mind, I always knew there was an old man back behind me on the beach, watching for me, trying to keep me in his sight as long as he could.

I hope my son always knows that as well. I also hope he always knows the Wiggle who played the guitar was the best.

Forever My Baby

I was an uncle for more than five years before I became a father.

I like to think being an uncle is a pretty good introduction into fatherhood. To at least one of my nephews I am "Big Unk." I am pretty proud of that moniker. It takes a lot of cool points to be a "Big Unk."

My father was an "Unk-Eye" to one of his nephews so I spent my entire life hearing the different nicknames for uncle.

If you don't understand both the pressures and prestige that come along with being any variation of "Unk" to one of your nephews, you're probably just a run-of-the-mill uncle.

My oldest nephew had the luxury – or curse – of having pretty much every family member on both sides of his family attend everything he did as a child, until other babies started making their appearance on the family tree.

So when it came time for him to graduate from Pre-K, he probably had more family members in attendance than I had when I graduated high school. He didn't have as many surprised family members as I had though.

I went with the rest of the family. If remember correctly, I went mocking all the pomp and circumstance involved. I am from the generation whose first experience with a cap and gown came in senior year of high school.

I figured it would be a cute little program. The kids would march out and stand on stage. Maybe sing the Barney song and a few others.

Some kids would probably cry on stage and at least one would do something during the program that might land him on "America's Funniest Home Videos." Then we would take some pictures and go out to eat with our family.

It looked like everything was playing out exactly as I had anticipated, right up until the teacher started to read the "I will love you forever, I will like you for always" book. That's when the program went off-script for me.

As I said, I was expecting a kid or two to cry when they looked out in the crowd from the stage and saw their parents. That was all the tears I was expecting at this soiree. Boy, was I wrong.

I don't think there was a dry eye in the house after the lady finished reading that book. I wasn't that emotional at my own graduation. I have been to funerals that weren't as sad as that Pre-K graduation.

They should have probably sung the Barney song before they read that book because there was no getting that crowd back at that point. Forget trying to take a picture with my nephew – I was looking for my mom in the crowd so I could hug her.

The book itself is beautiful. I'm not saying anything bad about it. I just think it should come with some kind of warning to new uncles going to their first-ever Pre-K graduation.

The daycares can put an asterisk at the bottom of the graduation flyer. Something to the effect of "FYI: you will probably be sitting in a plastic chair that stands no higher than 12 inches off the floor, and also, we will be reading the 'Forever My Baby' book, so bring plenty of tissues."

Want to save lives? Slow down

Want to save lives? Slow down

I once went up to a road where we had two speed-related fatalities in the not so distant past.

I was still pretty new to patrol, so everything was fresh and exciting. I told myself I was going to go set up on this road, write a few citations and word would get out to everyone in the area to drive the speed limit.

That's not quite how it worked out for me. I sat there for about three minutes, which was enough time for 2-3 cars to pass me. I could see from their taillights as they got off in the distance they were flashing oncoming cars to alert them that I was waiting up ahead.

So, every car that passed me was pretty close to doing the exact speed limit. I get it, drivers saving drivers from getting a citation. I used to flash cars, too, before I became a deputy. Then I worked a couple of fatality scenes where speed and/or alcohol were contributing factors.

Now, in the grand scheme of things, I was there to get people to slow down. And as long as I sat there and people were flashing their lights at one another to warn of my presence, then I was indeed getting people to slow down. Mission accomplished.

The problem is, that's only effective at slowing down cars for as long as I'm there. As soon as I drive away and people stop flashing their lights at each other, cars resume their normal speeds on that road.

Not long ago, around 11 p.m., 911 gave out a call about a vehicle swerving badly coming toward town. I wasn't far away from the location, so I went and set up where I would be able to intercept the suspect car as it approached.

I had no more gotten myself in position when I saw a vehicle matching the description – provided by the caller – pass me. I got behind it and, almost immediately, it swerved over both the fog line and the double yellow lines into the opposite lane.

I pulled the car over and ended up arresting the driver for driving under the influence. I was on the side of the road for maybe 20 minutes, I'm not certain. As I was on the side of the road there was a steady stream of traffic passing by us. I didn't think much of it – there are always cars moving in this county.

After I dropped the driver off at jail, I checked my phone and saw I had a text from my son. He was asking me if I had a car pulled over on the side of the road. He was on his way home from work and passed by me while I was on that traffic stop. He texted me when he got home, asking if it was my blue lights he had passed.

What that means is that particular car I had pulled over for crossing over the double yellow lines into the opposite lane was heading toward my son, who was coming home from work. Their paths could have crossed each other, if not for that 911 caller.

That night, on that street, it could have been my child. But we all have friends and family who travel these roads. It could have been your child, or your spouse, on a road heading toward a driver who was crossing into the oncoming lane of traffic.

That 911 caller saw something, and he said something. And in doing so, he may have very well saved multiple lives that night. Thankfully for me, I knew who the caller was and was able to personally thank him for calling 911 that night and helping get that driver off the roads.

Ride home from the beach

Thanks to a really good deal, we were able to take an impromptu trip to the beach a few weeks ago.

Usually on any family trip, I get to our destination as quickly as possible, making as few stops as necessary. Because I was trying to savor every moment of this trip, I paid more attention to the journey.

I didn't drive any slower, but I did make a few extra stops. We stopped at the Florida line and got a sample of grapefruit juice. All the times I have ever been to Florida and I had never done that before. It was delicious.

On the ride home, I noticed a car with Alabama tags pretty early in our trek. I only noticed it because it had a weird trailer hitch. I didn't think much of it, assuming we would drift apart after a few miles and never see each other again.

For whatever reason, this car and I stayed together mile after mile after mile. He would pass me for a few miles. Then I would pass him for a few miles.

We found ourselves stuck behind the drivers who drive the same speed right beside each other, not allowing anyone to pass. Anyone who has ever driven the roads to the Gulf Coast knows the drivers I'm talking about.

In the few instances where it drops down to one lane and you get a passing lane every few miles, he would stay behind me through the passing lane. That means he had grown to trust me.

There is a lot of pressure that comes with being the lead car in a passing zone. If he chooses to stay behind me and we go back to one lane, I feel like I need to repay his trust. I can't slow down and become one of those drivers who speeds through the passing zone but then resumes a normal speed on the one lane road.

I don't want to be that guy. I can't stand that guy.

I began to wonder about this new traveling companion of mine. What was his name? Where was he going? I figured he was on way to a Boy Scout Jamboree. That would explain the weird trailer hitch.

I know that the hitch and the Boy Scouts had nothing to do with one another, but since I was making up his identity and I wanted him to be en route to a Jamboree then that's exactly where he was going. He would have made it to Eagle Scout if he had gotten his Citizenship Merit Badge.

You can get pretty creative when you are inventing personas on a four and a half hour drive.

I named him Carl Morgan. That's a good name for a guy with an Alabama tag and a weird trailer hitch who was on his way to a Boy Scouts Jamboree. I saw him first in Florida and lost him somewhere down in Columbus.

I don't know where the lake is in Columbus where the Boy Scouts meet, but I trust he got there safely. He was a good driver. We spent a few hours on the road that day and didn't have the first kerfuffle.

Pecan trees and memories

I planted two pecan trees this weekend in our yard.

If we are lucky, within 4-5 years we should start getting a new form of free food here at the house. I cannot wait to pick up the first pecan from one of those trees. I wish I had planted these trees the first year we moved way out here to God's Country.

There were two pecan trees in the yard where I grew up. I didn't appreciate it at the time. I don't know how old these trees were, but I know they were very much mature based on the number of pecans that would fall in the yard. More than you could ever pick up, no matter how much you tried.

I'm convinced my maternal grandmother, Nanny Cook, was sure that leaving a pecan on the ground to rot was a sin. Now that I am grown and see how much pecans cost in a grocery store, I think she was probably right.

But I had way too much on my young plate to be worried about pecans in the yard. There was a probably a kickball game going on nearby that needed to be won. Or an episode of "The Flintstones" I was missing. But I knew better than to ever tell Nanny no if she asked me to go pick up pecans.

I don't mean not saying no out of fear. I don't recall ever getting a single whipping from her. Of course, I also don't recall ever deserving one, either. I have heard stories from my older brothers and cousins that she had it in her, the ability to dole out the corporal punishment. I've just always assumed they, rightly, had it coming.

I filled many a plastic grocery bag full of pecans for Nanny Cook in my childhood. Of that, I am proud. Ninety percent of those bags I filled were probably done so with a frown on my face. Of that, I am not so proud.

I didn't appreciate the yard I was growing up in was trying to give us free food, in the form of pecans. Nor did I comprehend that Nanny Cook would not always be around to ask for 10 minutes of my time.

Time she shouldn't have had to ask for. A chore I should have done just because I knew she wanted it done.

Planting these trees this weekend is hope that someday in the near future I will be leaning over filling up plastic grocery bags with pecans. Only this time I will have a smile on my face and a memory of someone in mind.

And who knows? Maybe I'll have enough pecans to fill two or three plastic grocery bags and, based on the current price point, pay off my house.

April Fool's Day and Easter

I figured I might try to be topical this week with both Easter and April Fool's Day coming up Sunday.

I think having Your friends show up at Your tomb only to be already gone up to Heaven ranks up there with the ultimate April Fool's Day trick, so it might me apropos that the two fall on the same day every once in a while.

I don't belong to a church. I don't go to church. I haven't been in years. That's not something I'm proud of. I wish I did. I should. I liked my life when I was active in church. It's a nice feeling, having hope in the afterlife.

Over the years I have run the gauntlet of excuses. My favorite would be: "Ah, some of the biggest hypocrites I've ever met were at church, that's why I don't go." That wasn't really true, it was just an excuse to make me feel better about not going.

But what if it were true? What if I had met some bad people at church? My favorite Bible verse has always been Mark 2:17: "On hearing this, Jesus said to them, "It is not the healthy who need a doctor, but the sick. I have not come to call the righteous, but sinners."

There are thousands of verses in the Bible, but that's my favorite. It always has been, and I suspect it always will be.

Jesus made a habit of hanging around with people the church didn't approve of. He hung with them because that's who He was here for. He's the Doctor, hanging out with the sick.

The word "Christian" literally means to be "Christ-like." So if He chooses to hang out with the sinners, the ones the church wants no part of, then who am I to act like someone can stop me from going to church to fellowship with like-minded Christians.

I wouldn't let an atheist from Wisconsin stop me from praying, anywhere and anytime I wanted to pray. So why should I let a church member I might not like stop me from going to church?

It's more about Who we go to church for, not who we go to church with.

If you believe what I am writing about, Happy Easter. When you show up for church on Sunday and see someone new sitting in that spot on the pew you sit in the other 51 weeks out of the year, smile at them, shake their hand and know – without a shadow of a doubt – the entire Reason you are even in that church building would very gladly spend His time with them.

They are probably already nervous enough about spilling the communion tray as it is passed around to be worried about if they are sitting in your spot.

If you don't believe in any of what I'm talking about, then I guess this column wasn't for you. Happy April Fool's day. I put $100 bills in all of the eggs I hid.

Uniform Colors

My work uniform is brown.

It is a heavy uniform to wear, both in the literal sense and in the figurative sense. I am approximately 40 pounds heavier in my uniform than I am out of it. Though it is not the most comfortable uniform in the world, I wear it with great pride.

My brown uniform allows me to work with the best people I have ever worked with in my life. With that being said, I am sometimes very fortunate to work with people who wear different colored uniforms.

Not long ago, I was dispatched to an unknown problem call close to the city. I was right around the corner from the location when it came out, so I was pulling onto the scene within 30 seconds to a minute of it being dispatched over the radio.

Within that time, all 911 could tell me was there was a gunshot victim inside the house and people screaming in the background. That's what I knew as I arrived.

What I also knew, based on my location, was there were probably not any brown uniforms within 3-5 minutes of me. That's a long time to wait for the Cavalry.

I entered the house and dealt with the "screamers in the background." I was able to determine the shooter was not at the scene. I then made my way to where they told me the gunshot victim was located.

As I was making my way through the living room, I looked out the window and saw a brother in blue coming through the yard to get to me. We can hear each other's radios, and he was close enough to me to make sure I wouldn't wait 3-5 minutes for backup.

As much as I love my brown, I was pretty happy to see blue that day. I hope the men and women in blue are equally as happy to see brown when we return the favor.

More recently than that incident, I received a call from a friend of mine who wears an even lighter shade of blue. We don't have access to each other's radio frequency, so cell phones are our mode of communication.

He called and asked me what area I was patrolling. When I told him, he gave me a vehicle tag and description to be on the lookout for that had been reported stolen from out of state.

I went to the area he told me it might be traveling and was able to locate it within a few minutes. I called him back and told him I had located the stolen vehicle and was following it. I kept him updated as to where I was as he made his way to me as quickly as possible.

Once he caught up to me, together, we stopped the vehicle and recovered it for the victim.

We may work for different agencies, and we may wear different-colored uniforms, but at the end of the day we all share the same mission: to protect our community. When push comes to shove, we play for the same team.

We will present a united front to anyone, or anything, that comes before us.

Jurisdictional lines are drawn on our maps, but they are not present anywhere in our hearts.

The difference between family and friends

I had a few things happen in my life last week which gave me pause to ponder.

First, I had some friends celebrate my birthday at Tower Place Crossfit. If you think the day after your 21st birthday was rough, I strongly recommend you try a crossfit birthday. It will make getting out of bed and successfully being able to walk a feat, without the bar tab and headache.

Be in the know the moment news happens

Next, I had a birthday party lunch with some of my best friends on earth. It was one of those three-hour lunches that still ended too soon because the company was so good. I think that's why people try to get by with celebrating their birthdays for a month. So they can have more lunches like I had the other day.

Then, my first-ever book was published last week. It's called "Columns I Wrote" and is available on Amazon and Kindle (shameless plug). I have another book that should be out within the next few months. Don't worry, I'll find a way to shamelessly add that title to a column as well.

Lastly, and most importantly, my mom spent seven days in the hospital last week. She gave us all quite the scare.

She is 72 and, as best as I can tell, had the kidney function of someone born in 1872, more or less.

I remember taking my oldest son to Newnan Academy for his first day of preschool. I gave him a kiss goodbye and turned around and walked away. I made sure not to look back because I didn't want to catch him crying and I didn't want him to see me tearing up.

I wasn't worried about catching my mother crying, but I didn't want her to see me tearing up. Not only was she not crying, she was probably still repeating "Well, if I had known they were going to keep me, I wouldn't have come down here." That had become her hospital mantra.

That's not what you expect to hear from someone who may very well have just had their life saved by a hospital. She would end up staying a week, having an emergency port put in her chest, along with several rounds of dialysis before she was finally able to come home. She will now continue dialysis.

But if you know my mother, you would know that in her head she felt fine and her being in the hospital might somehow inconvenience someone in her family. You would understand her skeptical grasp on her health issues.

I have always assumed that first preschool goodbye walk would be the hardest goodbye walk an adult would ever have to make. Last Thursday proved that theory wrong. Leaving the hospital that first night was 10 times worse than that preschool walk I made years ago.

I say "family," "friends" and "coworkers" a lot when talking about the people in my life.

Between the birthday celebrations, people reaching out wanting to buy a book ("Columns I wrote," even less shame this time) and everyone texting me asking about my mother showed me the line between the three is not as visible as I sometimes think.

When you have the right friends, coworkers and family, I don't think you need to specify the difference between the three.

I have an amazing family; there are no other specifications needed. Last week was a good reminder of that.

Whose streets? Our streets!

Friday afternoon: As I headed into the briefing I knew very little about what was going to happen Saturday. I knew I was on "Team Echo" and we would be "Greenville Street front line."

I also knew the chaos and destruction the groups coming Saturday have brought to other cities around the country.

One of the first things my Major said was, "Tomorrow is hands-on. If you have a problem with going hands-on, you better get over it before you report tomorrow."

Don't take that to mean we were out looking for a fight, it was quite the opposite. He reminded us that we would work under the same three rules we work with every day: Be nice, be nice and be nice.

He can only protect us if we do right. If we do wrong, we are on our own. We know that.

But we also know when you are dealing with aggressive and violent people you have to show them quickly that you are both prepared and capable to meet their aggression and violence with superior aggression and violence.

He then went on to remind us that, no matter what we believed personally, we had to uphold the Constitution.

As he relayed our plan for the next day, it didn't take long to realize whoever had come up with the plan had come up with a seemingly flawless plan. It would be up to us to execute it.

One important reminder he gave with an event like this: a high number of arrests doesn't mean it was a successful day. Conversely, the lower the arrests, the more successful our day would be.

The next time you are near Greenville Street Park, look how many different directions you can walk into and out of that park: All the roads leading in and around it, the areas between the buildings, the train tracks and woods.

We had to keep two groups separated that did not want to be separated.

Saturday morning: One of my favorite social media posts I saw that morning was from a friend of mine and it said: "The wolf is at the door, it's time to do what sheepdogs do."

We were ready for this day. We didn't want it in our town, but it was in our town and we were about to handle it.

I saw my Major and told him how good I thought our briefing was the day before. He said the hardest part for him was standing up there talking to us knowing that some of us may not get through the next day unharmed.

My team reported to our post on Greenville Street around noon. That was just enough time to make sure I was painfully sunburned before the day really began.

One radio report said a group was walking down Jackson Street heading for the park. The next report told us that many cans of hornet spray had just been purchased from local hardware stores.

We were then reminded that hornet spray will shoot up to 20 feet and is flammable.

That's not the most comforting radio traffic I've ever heard. Especially as I looked at the 1-foot barrier that would separate us from however many hundreds of people made it into the area.

I took solace in the fact there were checkpoints in place, and I knew I trusted the men and women posted at them.

The event happened. Many people entered through our checkpoints and they held their signs and screamed as loud as they could and hoped their voices would be heard. Those people made me proud and I assume were mostly local.

We could see quickly who was there with good intentions and who was there with bad intentions. Body language is more telling than most realize.

The problem was not with the people who came to protest the right way. The problem was the people who spent the day trying to get around our checkpoints. You can refer back to the newspaper article earlier in the week that shows some of the items we confiscated.

It could have gotten very ugly, very quickly, had some of those items made it inside the area.

At the end of the day, we had zero fatalities, zero injuries, zero dollars in property damage and only 10 arrests. That's a success.

After the long day was over, we were told St. Smyrna church had dinner waiting for us. We received a warm welcome and meal from a loving congregation. And seats, they had seats! We were ready to sit down.

Sunday morning: I was tired and ready for the shift to be over before it began. A small group of us met for breakfast at Cracker Barrel, where a gentleman paid for our breakfast as a kind gesture.

I was then asked to stop by South Metro Church with a few others so the congregation could invite us on stage to thank us.

I think I was more nervous on stage in church than I was Saturday. They were wonderful people and I was lucky to represent my agency in such a way. But the main thing on my mind was not falling up or down the stairs leading to the stage. Thankfully, I did not.

For lunch, I ran through the drive-thru at Taco Bell. The guy took my card and turned around and said something to his manager. She came into view, took the card from his hand and gave it back to me as she thanked me.

More people waved to me in my patrol car than normal on Sunday. More people shook my hand. It felt nice. It felt like we had just won the Super Bowl and were returning home.

Then I remembered what state I lived in and quickly snapped myself out of that daydream.

Sunday reminded me of how important it was that Saturday went exactly how Saturday went. People could have come to our town and destroyed it then left to go back to wherever they came from, leaving us to rebuild.

I think our community was scared going into this. I was. I wasn't worried about my personal safety. I knew who I worked for and with. I was more worried about damage to the town square my children grew up on.

On Sunday, everyone was relieved. And everyone went out of their way to show me they appreciated us.

None of the ridiculous things we were called on Saturday mattered to me or anyone else I work with. We encountered the people we encountered on Saturday for the people we encountered on Sunday, and every other day of the week in this town.

Those people may not be in any photographs you will see from Saturday, but we know they are there beside us and behind us. They are why we do what we do.

Parent Steps

Another school year is winding down. I will have a high school senior and a middle schooler next year. I know it's a tired cliché, at this point, to talk about how time flies. But any parent can tell you clichés are clichés because they are true, and time flying when you're a parent is all too sad but true.

A baby step is defined as "a tentative act or measure that is the first stage in a long or challenging process."

I am here to contend that a "parent step" is much more challenging of a process than a "baby step."

All the stages a baby goes through are exciting and cause for celebration. First they learn how to crawl. Then they learn how to walk. You send them off to school and sit back in amazement at how quickly they grow.

Sometime during high school is when the fun and exciting baby steps end and the sad and dreadful parent steps begin.

It begins with a job, or for me it has. They get their first job and you realize how quiet the house is the nights they work. I don't like a quiet house. A quiet house is an empty house. Parent steps.

I like noise and chaos. Unless I'm watching an old episode of "Hee Haw." Then I'm OK with silence for at least thirty minutes.

Once they get their first job, they start sleeping in a little later on the weekends. Going to school full time and working part time is a daunting schedule.

Then they find someone to date. So now your house is quiet on nights they are working and it's quiet on nights they're off because they are out on a date. Parent steps.

The most difficult parent step for me so far has been this past weekend. We were lucky enough to get a quick trip down to the beach. My son stayed home. So this was the first time in 17 years we have been to the beach without him.

The beach was still beautiful and the company was still awesome. But something was missing. Alvin's Island didn't look as inviting. The oysters didn't taste quite as good without him there to share. Parent steps.

It's the first time in my life I have ever been at the beach and was ready to come home.

I am not a guy who is looking forward to an empty nest. There is certainly nothing wrong with anyone who does. That's probably the more normal approach, it's just not how I'm wired I guess.

At the risk of sounding insulting to the missus when I am not trying to, I don't want to take a vacation with my wife, as just a married couple. Not because I don't love being her husband but because I don't want to take a vacation as anything other than "Dad."

We are, "Nix, table for four." That sounds much better than "table for two."

That's a pretty dramatic leap there, but it goes with the point I am trying to make. I know this is all part of the process. I was 17 once and I stayed home while my parents went on vacation. I get it. I just don't like it. Parent steps.

Each parent step we take is preparing us for our children to leave and go take on the world as we have raised them to do. That's the natural order of things.

If they went directly from, "Help me tie my shoe," to, "Hey, I'm heading off to college," it would be too much to handle at once. We have to take these parent steps as they come. No matter how much we may not like each step.

Aunt's Day

I'm almost positive I wrote a nice column last year for Mother's Day. And in it, I am certain I waxed poetic about both my mother and my children's mother. You would be hard pressed to find a better pair of mothers.

Since whatever I said last year will still apply this year, I have no Mother's Day column.

I do believe I have the next best thing however, a story about aunts. I am operating under the assumption that in some ancient language, the word "aunt" means "second mother." Which is exactly what my aunts have been to me.

My first memory of the aunt who is serving as the subject of this column is hearing her scream from across the street when I was a child. My grandmother lived across the street from us and my aunt would visit from time to time. These visits would sometimes fall on a Sunday when the Falcons were on TV.

There is no bigger Falcons fan on the planet than my aunt, and anyone who lived on our street and heard my aunt cheering for those Bartkowski Falcons, lo those many years ago, would not disagree.

Truth be told, I don't remember if I actually remember hearing her yell at the TV or if the story is family folklore at this point, but I don't think she would argue with this part of the story.

I remember when myself and the missus were starting out in our life together we didn't have two nickels to rub together. Twenty plus years later and that's still the case, but I digress.

We moved out to Douglasville which is also where my aunt lives. Neither my wife nor I liked the prospect of starvation so we would often find ourselves having dinner at my aunt's house.

If you remember from past writings, my aunt is one of only three people in my life who cook edible cornbread (my mother and my wife being the other two), so having dinner at her house was usually the best seat in town back then.

Not only would we eat until we could barely move, we would never leave without bags full of leftovers and anything else she thought we might need to hold us over until our next visit.

Southern hospitality at its finest.

I have always wanted to thank her for those dinners, and those memories. Hopefully this column will serve as a thank you, though many years late.

This past weekend, I was selling books on the town square for Market Day when I looked up and saw my aunt walking towards me. She had come all the way from Douglasville to see me. She had already bought five copies of my book, but still came down to say hi and have our picture taken.

She may have had something else to do while she was down here, but since it's my story, she came down only to see me.

Parents have to act like they are proud of you, it's what they signed up for. The same goes for spouses. But when an aunt says she is proud of you, she means it. She doesn't have to pretend. She has kids of her own she's busy being proud of.

Next time hallmark is looking to invent a card buying holiday, I think "Aunt's Day" should be in contention. I'll buy the card which has "You gonna eat your cornbread?" on the cover.

Turtle on a fencepost

A few years ago I was at a statewide convention being held in Athens, Georgia. It was my first, and only, time ever being there and I fell in love with the city. I'm still a Tech fan, don't get me wrong. I don't get invited to many conventions, so that may be my only time ever visiting Athens.

A guy who had just been elected to serve another year as the "high person" of the "some agency" got up to speak to the dinner crowd. I wonder if I don't get invited to many conventions because of my lousy memory when it comes to people, titles and agencies.

But one of the first things he said to us that night was that he was the epitome of the "turtle on a fencepost" analogy. Though I am sure this is an old and well-known analogy, I had never heard it.

He went on to explain that if you ever see a turtle perched on a fencepost you can be fairly certain it did not climb up there by itself. Someone helped it up there.

That's how he explained himself in his position with whatever the agency. He had not made it by himself, rather he had received plenty of help along the way.

That analogy has stuck with me all these years and it really hit home for me this past week. I am writing this on Wednesday and I can count no less than five different times since Monday that someone I work with has gone out of their way to help me out.

In each case, they had absolutely nothing to gain from than helping me. They gave up their time freely and their knowledge readily.

And in every instance, the help I received was very beneficial to me. I know who they are and they know who they are. I am not going to name names or give specifics here.

Mostly because I am going to take all the credit for every bit of help they gave me and also hope that anyone who may ever interview me for a promotion does not read this particular column. I will claim to be the world's first fence-jumping turtle.

I jest. I believe (and hope) I let everyone know how grateful I am for all the help I am ever given.

My entire life I have been a turtle- and I don't mean just because I'm pretty slow in a footrace.

I am a turtle on my personal fencepost. I am a turtle on my professional fencepost. And, assuming there are no misspellings or grammatical errors in this column, I am even a turtle on my literary fencepost (Thanks, editor who will remain anonymous.).

I hope in turn that I have helped a few turtles up on some fenceposts in my lifetime. But not real turtles, just hypothetical ones. I can't tell the difference between a nice turtle and a snapping turtle with a short fuse.

The end of an era

My youngest daughter will be done with elementary school today. Come August, that will leave me with a high school senior and a middle-schooler.

I took a day off work so I could go over to Ruth Hill Elementary for her last award ceremony. It has been a very good school for both my kids. After her ceremony, I'll check her out and let her pick what she wants for lunch.

One year we went for pedicures as an end-of-year treat but she never asked for that again. I'm fine with that. My feet are way too ticklish. I spent the entirety of my pedicure trying not to kick the lady while also apologizing to her for almost kicking her.

If my daughter is anything like her older brother, this was the last year for things like stopping by and having lunch with her. Middle-schoolers are way too cool to have their parents show up and cramp their style. That was my experience anyway.

I still remember her kindergarten award ceremony. I remember the pride I felt when some stranger walked up to us and said, "What have you done to have her so far ahead?" That pride was immediately followed by anger when I realized that stranger was talking to my wife and not me. But in all honesty, she was asking the right person.

I think now the big thing is to have the kids do a farewell walk through the halls of the school as conquering warriors. We didn't do that back in my day, but back in my day we were tired from walking to school- uphill both ways.

Or maybe we did and I was just never invited to do so because I was too busy doing make up work trying to get my grades up at the last minute, I'm not positive.

Assuming they do walk through the halls one last time before they head off to middle school, I will be there along the wall ready to capture a video of her walking by. I'll post it all over social media, as if my child is the first to accomplish such a feat. I will expect you to click "Like" on the video and comment something as to how she sure is a chip off the old block.

As I am capturing the video I will probably tear up a little. I am much more sentimental now than I was when her older brother was going through all these motions. I didn't appreciate how quickly everything was happening back then.

But being the man's man that I am, I will need to remind all the others in the hallway how rough and tough I am. I will probably try to blame the pollen for my eyes watering up. I hope they buy it.

As much as I hate to have these moments pass by so quickly, I love that I am lucky enough to be a part of them.

Oh, the humanity

I like to think most of my columns are written in good spirits, with the hope they may leave the reader, assuming there is one, in a better mood than they found him in.

But my air conditioning went out earlier in the week and it's June in Georgia. The inside of my house has been hotter than the outside of my house for several days now. I think whoever built this house insulated it with whatever they coat the walls of an oven with.

For that reason, this column is being typed with as much ill-tempered heat exhaustion that I can muster. I will use this 600-word space I am given to angrily weep and gnash my teeth about the woes of being hot 24/7. I may try to fit in an "oh the humanity" reference if I have room at the end.

I grew up in a house with no air conditioning right up the road in Union City. At the moment, I have no idea how I survived one Georgia spring, let alone many Georgia summers.

My bedroom window stayed open most of the year, with a box fan on high seated securely on the window ledge. The combination of the box fan and all the noises that come from Southern outdoors made for tranquil sound effects, but it did little to stifle the Georgia heat.

I still remember when we got our first window unit. I was in my teens. It went in the living room window, right beside the front door. Walking from any room in the house to the living room was like walking from a furnace to a meat locker.

I think we had five living in the house when we got that window unit. I slept on the living room floor, as privacy was not as important as making sure I was in that meat locker as much as humanly possible. I'm almost positive I was not the only one sleeping in the living room.

I remember when we got a second window unit a few years later. That unit went in the kitchen window, near the back door. Now we had two rooms in the house you would walk into without risking a heat stroke.

We were 1980s Redneck Royalty. You know how good a popsicle tastes in the summer when you have the luxury of eating it slow enough to actually taste it? Not just scarfing it down as fast as possible so it doesn't melt all over your fingers? You couldn't tell us anything.

To this day, I have no idea how I never opened the front door to find Robin Leach standing there with a camera crew. Hollywood hadn't made its way east yet is all I can figure.

I can only assume we survived all those summers without air conditioning because we didn't know what we were missing. It's possible to go from not having air conditioning to having it.

I do, however, contend it is impossible to go from having air conditioning to not having it. I offer up my internal body temperature for the last few days as Exhibit A.

I can't do it. I don't want to do it. I wonder if I move to Alaska if I could still send my weekly column down here for publishing. Because if I have my way, this is the last column I ever type with a wet wash rag draped over my head. Oh, the humanity.

There. I knew I could get it in before the 600th word.

Red light, Blue light

I write about my job a good bit. I love the work I do, the agency I work for and the community we serve. So it's an easy topic to write about.

The first column I ever wrote was about my years at 911 Dispatch and some of the craziness that comes along with that job.

Not long ago, I wrote about the men and women who wear different shades of blue uniforms I am lucky enough to know and work with.

For no good reason, I have never written much about the men and women who run into danger using red lights instead of blue.

I hope I never need any service they offer, but if I am in need, I am glad to know it's them coming.

Much like I can't imagine a better agency to work for, I can't imagine a better agency to work with. Our fire department is second to none.

They train with us. When we have active shooter training, they have active shooter training.

They are there with us, hoping we never need the skills we are honing, but knowing that should it ever come to us, we are prepared.

We know, should something really bad ever happen to us at work, it's them who are coming to save us. And we are more than comfortable with that knowledge. We know them.

Their leaders teach us emergency first aid. They give us tools and knowledge we need to survive.

Last week I was working an accident on the interstate, one of the aspects of the job I enjoy the least. Too many people don't see the need to slow down or move over.

No more than six or seven months ago, my shift was working a wreck on the interstate when a car-rear ended a fire truck that was on scene with us.

The fire truck was by far the largest and most visible vehicle on the interstate, along with the most lights flashing, yet a car happened to run into it at full speed, while three first responders stood on the other side of it working.

So back to last week, I'm on the interstate working an accident. The injured have been taken away in an ambulance. The lanes have been cleared. All I had to do was wait for the wrecker to come tow the wrecked vehicle.

The fire department's job was done. It was 3:00 in the morning (keep in mind, they work 24-hour shifts). There was nothing left for them to do on that scene, they could have left and gone back to the station.

But they stayed on scene with me, with their big red truck and all the flashing lights, blocking us from all the traffic that doesn't see the need to slow down or move over.

I didn't ask them to, but I sure was glad they did. And it was a pleasant conversation to boot.

We may run to a scene under a different color light, but make no mistake, we are one team.

Beeline

In the past week I have pulled between 10-15 gallons of honey from beehives and filtered it down for sale, as local and raw as I can provide.

I also didn't mow my lawn at all this year until the day after I robbed the hives of their honey. My yard has a ton of clover, so though bees can travel up to three miles a day for food, I can say with confidence that my honey is a whole lot of wild clover honey.

I posted a picture of the first batch of honey we bottled on my social media and the response from friends was amazing. I sold out within a few hours. I shipped some honey to friends and family in both Florida and California.

I had two offers from local business owners on the town square to sell my honey in their stores. They have also offered to sell my book, but that's a shameless plug for another column.

My honey costs more than the honey you can buy in the store. I understand that. But from how quickly I sold out of the first batch, I think people also understand how rare it is, in this day and age of GMO's and hormones in everything we eat, to be able to know where something on our dinner plate has come from.

I can show you pictures of my hives, along with pictures of my bees working flowers in my yard. If you are a friend of mine on social media, you have seen those very pictures, probably ad nauseam at this point. But the entire process fascinates me still, three years after I bought my first hive.

The money I will make on honey this year will be what allows me to take my family to the beach this summer. Now, as far as Toby Nix Beekeeping Incorporated goes, I am still pretty deep "in the red" from buying all the hives and equipment three years ago – and a little more equipment each year.

But for the first time, this year, I have enough honey to sell. And the hives and equipment I bought three years ago are the same hives and equipment I hope to be using three years from now, so I'm calling this year a profit.

It's the time of year you will see lots of local and raw honey on local store shelves. I can't speak for any other beekeeper as to what they spend and what they make, but I think I can speak for them when I say any money they make from honey is going to pay a bill they owe, or maybe help finance a family trip. Or, at the very least, to buy more equipment in the hopes of getting more honey next year.

No chain store offered to sell my honey. Locally owned shops on our town square offered. They are in the same shape I am in. The money they make goes to their bills, their vacations, reinvesting in their shops for future growth.

Actually, I take that back. I have a day* job (*figuratively at the moment). They don't have a day job to fall back on. Go downtown and walk around the shops. Look how many locals they are supporting on their shelves. They invest in us, their community. We need to always do everything we can to invest in them.

Still winning

The date: June 21, 1997

The location: Buffington Road Christian Church, College Park.

The setting: I had somehow convinced a lady way too pretty for me to marry me.

I don't know if she had really poor vision, or really bad taste in men, but since I was the beneficiary of whatever it was, I was keeping quiet.

I was 21. She was three months older than me, which means she was practically robbing the cradle. A fact I try to remind her of as often as possible. Maybe it was her advanced age that can explain her poor vision.

I stood up in the area in front of the pulpit waiting for her to walk down. I don't know what other guys think about but I can tell you all I was thinking about was not passing out. I kept reminding myself to keep my legs bent enough to let blood flow through them.

I had seen enough "America's Funniest Videos" by this point to assume someone fell out at every wedding. I didn't have enough hair for it to get set on fire by a random candle so my only concern was not falling and not flubbing a line.

Neither my wife to be nor I cared much for public speaking, or pomp and circumstance, so we told the Preacher to say only what he legally had to say to make us official. I think the video will show, from the moment she walked down the aisle to the moment we walked back up it as a married couple, only 17 minutes had passed. That was 16 minutes too long, but I know Les Shell (best Preacher ever) had given us what we had asked for.

The only thing he didn't concede on was the bride wanted to walk down the aisle to "Nothing else Matters" by Metallica. He balked at that, but I still contend it's the perfect wedding song.

I made it through the wedding without falling down or catching anything on fire, so the day was a success to me.

We proceeded down to the church's fellowship area for the after wedding party. My mom and aunt had prepared enough Southern food to feed an army. Her family had prepared enough Cambodian food to feed a similar-sized army. I distinctly remember her father carrying in huge bowls of fresh made eggrolls. Our post-wedding party was a feast for the ages.

Our families provided all the food. We didn't have to pay for the church because we were members there. Les Shell married us for free for the same reason, and because he was the greatest Preacher ever. My sister-in-law served as the photographer because she knew what all pictures needed to be taken.

We paid maybe $300.00 for her wedding dress. I don't know if that's good or bad, but it looked good on her. I rented a tux for $99.00 from Shannon Mall. As far as I can recall, that's still the last time I have worn a tie that was not against my will.

I don't know how much money she had to spend on nausea medication that day, but given who she was marrying, it may have been a good bit. I still think we made out for under $500.00 total. That's not a bad deal. Not that there is anything wrong with big weddings, it's just what we preferred.

I knew I was lucky that day. Twenty-one years later and I am still realizing just how lucky I was. Don't tell her I said that though.

Also, she forgot our anniversary this year, so I am entering into a one-year automatic argument win streak. It's the best anniversary gift a man could ask for.

My priorities are perfectly straight

I just booked a condo for us to go on vacation soon. The white sands of the gulf are my happy place. My place to recharge and unwind.

Was it the most financially wise thing to do? No. There are several different bills I could put this trip money to that would elevate me to "responsible adult" status. But who ever looked back over their life and reminisced about a bill they paid lo those many summers ago? I have a 17- and an 11-year-old and we all need to see the beach.

Escapism is defined as the tendency to seek distraction and relief from unpleasant realities, especially by seeking entertainment or engaging in fantasy.

Now, I am in love with my reality. I have a home, family and friends I love. But the fantasy for me is that maybe, someday, we will own a place of our own looking over the white sands of the Gulf.

My son is about to enter his senior year of high school. He has a job and works 4-5 days a week most weeks. This trip can be five days where he can take off work and not think about whether he is going to join the military or what colleges he may be interested in.

My daughter starts sixth grade and will be in a new school where she doesn't know anyone. She is excited, but nervous. Though her choices may not be as life-defining as military or college, deciding what sport you want to play or what school club you want to join surely weighs heavy on an 11-year-old mind.

I love my job, but any chance I get to take a few days off from wearing a 35-pound uniform during the business end of a Georgia summer, I'm happy to take it.

My wife will spend 5 days having to look at me in a bathing suit. I don't pack many shirts or socks for a beach trip. She will also have to smear sunblock on my back since I come from a long line of skin more suited for life around the arctic than the equator. With those few things in mind, her mental escape will probably come after our vacation, when I am back at work, in full uniform.

I will always choose to make memories with my family when I get the chance. The bills will be there waiting on me. The kids will be out on their own, making memories with their families someday. And it seems like I get a new reminder every week of just how soon that day will be upon me, no matter how much I dread it.

I wonder if this mentality is why my career as a financial advisor never took off. I bet I would make a great memory advisor though. "Memory Help 5 cents. The doctor is in."

A "Charlie Brown" reference from a man in his 40s. You would never get that from a guy who was current on all his bills.

I love you, too

Any time I leave the house I kiss the family goodbye. I have never liked saying goodbye while angry, but the day I was given a bulletproof vest as part of my work uniform I vowed to never have any "bad goodbyes."

Based on the hours I'm leaving the house, I do more than my fair share of saying goodbye while they are still sleeping.

When I lean down and say, "I love you," both of my kids will say "I love you, too." "I love you, too" is not an unusual response to "I love you," but what I find so fascinating about it is they will say "I love you, too" without really even waking up.

I have done a lot of things wrong during their lifetime, but I know both of my children are conditioned to say "I love you, too" without fully waking up.

I am not conditioned that way. I have much less faith in humanity. If something wakes me up, I am seeing just how quickly I can eliminate whatever it is.

I don't know how my wife is conditioned to respond when she is awakened. Truth be told, I have never had to wake her up to tell her goodbye because I could never successfully leave the house without her being awake and helping me find one thing or another.

I'm not even certain she sleeps. She has a pillow, but I can't confirm she has ever had to buy a replacement pillow.

Several years ago, when my son was much younger and I was much more dumb and selfish, I was gone more than I should have been.

I remember falling asleep on the living room sofa one night and him falling asleep on the floor right beside the sofa.

I think he fell asleep there because he wanted to know if I got up to leave. There is no way I could have gotten off the sofa without tripping over him. That's one of those memories that is burned in my brain no matter how badly I wish it wasn't.

He forgave me for that phase of my life long before I ever forgave myself, assuming I have forgiven myself at all.

That's the joy of family. They will forgive you. They will forget about it. And they will be so sound in their sleep, and in their knowledge of your love for them, that they don't even have to be fully awake to know that you are there beside them and you are there with love.

I hope they always sleep so soundly. I hope they always know they are loved.

And I hope they can one day answer the question as to whether or not their mother does indeed sleep, because I don't think I will ever be able to.

Deep breaths

Deep breath in, deep breath out. This is why we train the way we train. That is the mantra I keep telling myself.

I have never trained for a vehicle chase, but I have Emergency Vehicle Operator Course (EVOC) training and I have trained for stressful situations.

My agency uses "stress inoculation" training throughout the year, every year. And I can't imagine any agency could do it any better.

I'm in my first vehicle pursuit. I knew it was coming. It was only a matter of time. When I started as a dispatcher for 911 I knew I would someday take a cardiac arrest call. It's the nature of the beast.

So when I became a deputy, I knew I would someday have foot chases. I knew I would one day be in a car chase. They happen in this line of work.

I work in a profession where confrontation is what we do. Whatever is presented to us, we confront it. Deep breath in, deep breath out. This is why we train the way we train.

The Supreme Court protects me, saying that "police officers are often forced to make split-second judgements - in circumstances that are tense, uncertain and rapidly evolving."

This is about as tense, uncertain and rapidly evolving as it gets.

My speedometer tells me we are going over 80 miles per hour. My brain tells me it's more like 35mph. I can't believe how slow everything looks out my window. It's as if the outside view and the speedometer are not in sync with each other.

Deep breath in, deep breath out. This is why we train the way we train.

He leads me and another deputy in the chase off the road and into the woods. Our cars were not designed to go off road, but they are going off road today.

He knows these woods, it is clear by the way he is making his way down these trails in his truck.

We aren't in the woods for more than a mile before he jumps out of his truck and starts running on foot. I've been in foot chases before. All I have to do is keep him in sight. He will gas out before I do.

He may be faster than me; most bipeds are. But this is why we train the way we train. Deep breath in, deep breath out. Keep him in sight and wait for him to exhaust himself.

The first thing I looked at when he got out and started running were his hands. I remember hearing about the officer not long ago who was in a foot chase and turned a corner, while running after the person, and was met with gunfire from the person he was chasing.

Are we chasing someone who has weapons in his hands? Or on his body somewhere? And if so, at what point is he willing to use them on us?

He just demonstrated on the road that he doesn't care about his safety, or the safety of anyone else. How far is he going to take this? I am wearing a body-worn camera just above my ear. It is recording all of this. I wouldn't work for an agency that didn't provide me with a camera.

I know if something bad happens to me on this chase, or any call, my wife and kids will see and hear the footage on the news.

I'm not a husband or a father to the media. I am whatever the agenda is. I am a good guy to those who like me and a bad guy to those who don't.

It's the world we live in. Deep breath in, deep breath out. This is why we train the way we train.

Stop and smell the bonsai

I always thought my father was crazy for stopping at different roadside stands while we were traveling to or from the beach.

Now, anyone who has ever met my father instantly knows this column is not going to end with a "boy, was I wrong" conclusion. At best, I may be able to make it more like a "maybe he isn't as crazy as I tell people he is."

As a traveler, I have always just wanted to get where I was going as quickly as possible, rather it be my vacation destination or home following vacation. We stop for gas when we have to and on really long car rides maybe run through a fast food drive-thru just so the kids don't start plotting any backseat mutinies on me.

I used to drive up to Washington, D.C. at least every few years. That's a 9-10 hour drive if I remember correctly. One year we stopped around halfway and spent the night in a motel.

All I could think about the entire time I was laying in the motel bed was where I would be on the highway had I stayed on the road.

My wife has always wanted to stop by one of those "side of the road" stands you pass on the way to the beach.

You know the stands. You'll pass an "Alligator Jerky 5 miles on right" sign. Then an "Ostrich Jerky 4.5 miles on right" sign. You keep seeing various "jerkied" animal signs.

In addition to the jerky, the signs start advertising different jellies and jams, fruits and vegetables and Tupelo honey right up until you zoom past a little stand that couldn't possibly fit all the stuff inside it that the five miles of signs just promised you.

I can't forget bonsai trees. They also sell bonsai trees at these stands. I know this because a) I have been at least mildly fascinated with bonsai trees since "The Karate Kid" came out and b) that's why my wife always wants to stop, for a bonsai tree.

There are only so many consecutive trips I can say, "Yeah, I don't think that one is open," as I drive past it, going the speed limit and speed limit only.

That excuse has worked longer than it should because we always leave so early in the morning.

Last week, as we were traveling home from the beach, I finally pulled into into one of these stands.

Not only did it have every item that the five miles of signs has promised, it had much more. Shelves upon shelves of local foods, complete with a little old lady to talk to us as we walked around.

We bought different kinds of honey from different kinds of fields. I still contend my honey tastes better. We bought Mayhaw jelly, after learning what a mayhaw was.

We also bought moonshine jelly, which tastes about like what you would expect moonshine jelly to taste like. That's not an endorsement to buy it, for any other reason than curiosity's sake.

The only thing we didn't buy was a bonsai tree. Which is what my wife has wanted – lo these many years of driving past these "closed stands."

It was a very pleasant stop. One we will plan on making each trip back from the beach.

Next time you're coming to the end of those five miles worth of signs, slow down, they may be open.

Maybe Pop isn't as crazy as I tell everyone he is. Maybe.

Sunday Suppers

I know that all regions of the country, and world, make wonderful family and friend memories around their dinner table.

But I am from the South, and I love being from the South, so I am going to write as if we are the only ones who do it properly, because we probably are.

The first thing we get right down here is knowing how to fry foods. We put a lot of faith in our cardiologists down South. I'm sure they are the best of the best, that's why they are down here to begin with.

The guys in medical school who excel in cholesterol-related health issues move down South much the same way the guys who excel in plastic surgery move to the West Coast. Supply and demand.

Like most Southern-born, Southern-bred folk, I remember plenty of Sunday lunches at the house growing up. I suppose I should refer to them as "Sunday suppers" if I am to remain true to form.

And like most others (I presume), our Sunday suppers were typically fried chicken and fried potatoes. Much like her cornbread, I would put my mother's fried potatoes up against anyone in any cooking competition.

The second thing we get right is we don't even need a dinner table. In fact, the kitchen table in my house holds more clutter and bills than it ever holds food anyway.

We make the vast majority of our good memories standing around and eating directly off a $200 grill. If we are feeling extra fancy we may put some paper plates and condiments on top of the cooler we don't use anymore but won't throw away. It makes an excellent makeshift table.

But we only pull out the paper plates when guests we want to impress show up.

The longer it takes for something to cook, the better. I love waking up in the middle of the night and putting meat on the smoker, knowing that by the time it's done later that evening I probably won't even be hungry.

I just enjoy having family or friends come and stand around the grill. If the company is good enough, the food doesn't have to be. Which does not mean the food isn't good, I'm an expert-level griller or my name isn't Toby Nix. I'm just lucky enough to keep really good company, which trumps any food.

After last week's column, I received an email from a lady who grows bonsai trees. She invited us over so she could introduce us to the world of bonsai trees. And like any true Southerner, she ended her email with "let me know when you're coming and I'll be sure to have a BBQ spread."

Which reminds me of the third thing we get right here in the South. We know that the word "barbecue" can be a noun or a verb, but usually a noun. If you ask me, "grilling out" is the verb that produces "barbecue" the noun.

I guess you could invite someone over to your house so you could barbecue some barbecue. Remember though, if you give them more than 3 days' notice you're probably going to have to break out the paper plates and mustard.

Southern patience

Another school year is starting back up, and it's the time for us to remember to show the same respect and compassion to those on the road who are still on this side of Heaven.

Once in a while, as part of my job, I will work a funeral escort.

I would say 99% of the cars stop and pull over to the side of the road as we pass. A lot of the older guys even take their hats off as they are pulling over. I'm old myself, so I take my hat off should I ever pass an escort on an off day.

I'm not sure what taking the hat off does, but it seems like the right thing to do.

There is always at least one person who ignores the entire procession and drives right on through everything.

The fact that he is unable to look anyone in the eyes as he does so shows he is ashamed, but has yet to come to terms with there being other people inhabiting his planet.

That one person notwithstanding, working funeral escorts always give me chills. It's a sad thing to be a part of, but it's also a beautiful reminder of our community. Watching a stranger's reaction to a family's sad day.

You can tell when they realize they are coming up on a funeral procession. Almost immediately, they will look in their rear view mirror to make sure they can safely slow down and pull over to the side of the road.

It may be a small gesture, pulling over and waiting for a procession of cars to pass. But it's a sign of respect, and compassion, and it's something else that I think we get right in the South.

We will have kids waiting for school buses on the side of the roads. Some kids will be crossing the roads to get to the bus stop.

There will be young drivers, nervously driving back and forth to school for the first time. They are young and inexperienced, tailgating them may lead them to drive faster than they are comfortable driving.

They haven't learned the appropriate response to a tailgater is to slow down to one mile per hour under the speed limit and keep that pace forever. Be patient with them. They will learn.

Leave a little earlier, drive a little slower and always remember: no matter where you work or what you do, there is always at least one person hoping you called out sick anyway. No need to hurry. Wherever you're going is going to be there when you get there.

Nowhere to go but up

A buddy of mine got engaged last week. I went and saw him the other night and he told me the story of how it all went down.

The amount of forethought and planning that went into pulling off the "popping of the question" was impressively in-depth, and well-executed.

As he told his love story, full of romance and surprise, it brought to mind another engagement story. This one is not so full of romance or surprise, or even much planning. I am pretty sure, if you asked the lady who was proposed to, she may just tell you it was full of something, however.

Anyone who knows me knows I am horrible at planning things. The fact that I still get invited to anything more than three hours in advance is a testament to how patient and loving my friends are.

I woke up one morning, many years ago, and decided I wanted to get engaged to the gal I had been dating since high school.

I went to a jewelry store that day to pick out a ring. I told the guy the price range I could afford, and after he got his hysterical laughing under control, he proceeded to show me some rings.

This is where we found out that I am as good at making financial decisions as I am at planning things.

This guy showed me a ring and said it was a flawless diamond. I had no idea what that meant. I'm not even certain the "WWJD" bracelets had been invented by this point, but that's about the only jewelry I have ever worn.

He handed me the ring and the little monocle thing they look through. He directed me to look through the diamond and see it had no lines in it. He then showed me the comparison, a flawed diamond, which I looked through and saw a line running through it.

In a decision that still baffles me to this day, I thought to myself, "Well, nothing is too good for my lady. I'm getting the flawless one."

So I did. But if I had been thinking clearly, for the same price I could have gotten her a diamond probably three times that size. None of our friends carry around those monocles to check the clarity of diamonds. Who cares if there is a little line on the inside?

The story gets worse. That's just me buying the ring. I still had to deliver it to its intended recipient.

In all my romantic glory, I went and bought her a card. I'm fairly confident it was some kind of love card, but for all I know it could have been a "Get well soon" or a "Happy Birthday" card. I don't remember.

I bought the card, and we are going to give me the benefit of the doubt and say it was a love card for the purposes of this story. I wrote "Will you marry me?" on the card and taped the ring (flawless, mind you) to the bottom of the card.

When I saw her later that day, I handed her the card and just stood there while she opened it. Thankfully for me, she said yes.

So fellas, if you think your engagement was kind of bad, let your wife read this one. She will see you in a whole new light, I'm sure.

I didn't set out to have a terrible proposal, I thought I was doing ok. But hindsight being 20/20 and all, I can see it was pretty bad.

On the bright side for me, there wasn't much downhill I could go from there. If I drop the ball on Valentine's Day or an anniversary, it's not like she can point back to some high spot of mine and say I've changed.

A loving reminder

"It was then that I carried you."

That's the last line of the poem, "Footprints in the sand." I'm sure legal reasons and word counts would prevent me from posting the entire poem in this column, so I would encourage anyone who has never read it to look it up. It's a beautiful poem.

For those of you who are familiar with it, I'm hoping you may appreciate this. I will preface this all by saying, I have, in no way, been going through any low or sad times. I love my life.

But I did recently go through a little stretch of being discouraged and/or frustrated. It was during that stretch I was reminded of the people I am lucky enough to be surrounded by.

Within the span of a few days, four different guys I work with said "I love you man" during random conversations. I was caught off guard by that initially. Outside of my wife and kids, I don't say "I love you" very often. Not that I don't love people, I just don't say it much (I don't say it ever, really).

Two of the guys who told me were leaders of mine, and two were peers. But they are all people I look up to, even though one of them is pretty short.

Because I don't say "I love you" to many people outside of my wife and kids, I also don't hear it very often outside of them. I don't feel unloved at all. It's just not something I say or hear much.

So when I hear it, it always throws me off a little. Just like when someone tries to hug me, I tend to make it awkward.

After I found myself in this unusual position of hearing it frequently, I thought about it: Grown men- men's men- were randomly saying they love me, as if something, or someone, let them know I needed to hear it.

Then I remembered the verse in the Bible: John 15:13- "Greater love has no one than this, to lay down one's life for one's friends."

There is no doubt in my mind, that is exactly the kind of love they have for me, even the short one. I've been on calls with them, I've trained with them. I trust them with my life, literally.

As if my work buddies coming through in the clutch wasn't enough of a reminder, I was at the gym the other day and was chatting with an older man in the locker room, awkwardly I'm sure. I went to leave and told him to have a good day, to which he replied, "Hey man, I love you and Jesus does, too."

Something, or someone, led that stranger to say that to me that day.

Like I said in the beginning, I love my life. And I wasn't going through anything bad. But when I was even just a little bit down, I had reminder after reminder of how lucky I am.

When I look back on my life, like the man in the poem did, there is no telling how many sets of footprints I will see. But I know for sure there will be many more than mine along the path.

High school reunions

My parents are in their seventies now and have a high school reunion every other year. I think they keep adding more and more graduating classes to the party, as the number of potential attendees decrease each year.

I graduated in 1994 from the best high school in the land (Creekside). In 24 years, I think we may have tried to have a reunion a few years ago. I'm not positive, if there was one, I didn't go.

I didn't care much for those four years. Nothing against anyone there, it just wasn't for me. I do like that I can keep up with schoolmates through social media. There are one or two I get to see in real life often, and several more who I would like to see.

I would probably go to a reunion after I made my first million dollars. But I am learning the old saying is true, the first million IS the hardest.

Even though high school wasn't my thing, I got yearbooks every year. I think I still have them tucked away in a closet somewhere.

I remember my senior pictures were a big deal. Trying to decide which one I picked to be in the yearbook. It was a tough decision because they were all equally pretty bad.

That haircut with the line, where the hair was short toward the neck and longer up top did not age very well at all.

I'll just call it what it was: It was a bowl cut.

I rocked a bowl cut most of the way through high school. No wonder my hair decided to leave my head. It was out of shame.

I also remember getting a class ring, which I still blame my wife for losing lo those many years ago. She says she didn't lose it, but I let her wear it and I also loaned her my Live "Throwing Copper" cassette tape. I haven't seen either one since.

I'm not one to hold a grudge, but that is still a pretty sore topic for me. It was a really good tape.

My son is a senior this year and it's been a completely different senior year than I remember. He has shown no interest in taking senior pictures or buying a class ring. I don't think he has gotten a yearbook since elementary school.

And unlike his father, he actually likes school. I guess his generation has enough ways to keep up with each other. There is no sense in senior pictures. Thanks to cellphones, his mother and I have taken well over a hundred thousand pictures of him at this point in his life, I'm sure.

Is this the new norm? Are other high school seniors not into the pomp and circumstance that I remember so (sort of) fondly?

I think it would be nice to go to a reunion. Maybe my parents will invite me to one of their reunions. I think with my hairline and my limp I could pass for a 1960s-era Fulton High graduate.

Football season

Depending on which newspaper you read, college football begins either tomorrow or last Saturday.

It's that magical time of year in the South when family and friends come together to hate each other for a few months for no other reason than what team they root for.

Usually, this time of year I confidently predict Georgia Tech will go undefeated and win the National Championship. I secretly hope that if they can't, then maybe they will at least lose enough games to get a new coaching staff. They typically land somewhere between my two wishes.

In 1990, Georgia Tech won a National Championship. It was a good year, 1990.

We had "Home Alone" and "Dances with Wolves" as blockbuster hits. "The Simpsons" aired on Fox for the first time in 1990.

In June, the demolition of the Berlin Wall officially began. I remember that well.

Tim Berners-Lee published his proposal for the World Wide Web in 1990. Without this proposal, we wouldn't be able to log into social media and know how everyone we have ever met in our life, and everyone we will never meet in our lives, feels about every polarizing topic on earth. Thanks Tim.

We have to go back much further to see when Georgia was a National Champion. The year was 1980.

Unlike 1990, 1980 was a much darker time. Which makes it a good year for Georgia to win the Championship. It lines up with the entire crummy year.

The Pony Express was coming into existence, making mail routes to the Pacific Coast much easier. That's kind of a good thing, I just want to set the stage for how long it's been since Georgia has won the Championship.

We had just come out of both an Ice Age and the Depression. The Titanic was preparing for its maiden voyage across the Atlantic. The Donner Party was packing up to head out west.

As if all that happening in one calendar year wasn't bad enough, on January 1, 1980, a black cloud formed over the Louisiana Superdome and Georgia beat Notre Dame 17-10 to become the National Champions.

In conclusion, just like in grade school math where the alligator eats the bigger number, I think we can all agree here that 1990>1980. I hope that alligator reference didn't open the door for any Florida fans to chime in.

Fret not my Bulldog loving pals. It could be worse. You could pull for a team from that state to the west of us.

2018 College Football season, let the smack talk begin. May all your teams go undefeated. Until they play the Yellow Jackets, of course.

Side note: I had a few people see me on a call this past week and introduce themselves to me after the work was done. We chatted for a few minutes. I also had a few people email me about some articles they liked. I don't think I will get such emails for this column, but I do want to thank you all who reached out to me last week. That's a special feeling, to be recognized, that I don't think I could ever get used to – or tired of.

Growing up (or pretending to)

Are the first 18 years enough time to prepare him for the next 18 years?

Eighteen years seems like a long time. But there is a lot to cram in. A lot of things have to be done right if he is going to be strong enough to take on the next 18 years.

It all happens so fast. The first few years are spent mastering the small things, crawling, walking and learning to tie shoes.

All the first days of school – the first few are tough but they get easier with each passing year. Around middle school is when it really starts to fly by. High school is a blur.

You always hear he has to have "the talk" like there is only one, but there are many talks to be had, all important in one way or another. All awkward in their own way.

The second 18 years will start off with college or the military, whichever he chooses. Then he will find his career path and start out his own life.

Each year he needs a little less help from his parents. The less help he needs, the better they have done in raising him. It's like it's a weird form of punishment for raising a child right, realizing they don't need you as much as you need them to.

If you think I am writing this out of concern for my son, as he enters his next 18 years, you don't know me – or him – very well. He will do great. I have no worries about how he will handle this next phase of life.

I'm worried about me. Have I spent these first 18 years preparing me for the next 18? I like a noisy house. I can't say I like a messy house, but I'll take it if includes noise and kids.

He doesn't need me to put together his toys anymore. He doesn't even need me to buy them anymore. OK, that last one is kind of nice, but still.

I told him the other morning as I drove him to have his wisdom teeth taken out, he has to be patient with his mother and me. We are having to learn to let go at the same time he is learning to be grown. Neither he nor we have been in this situation before. It's not easy on any of us.

I don't know how my parents did it. By the time I was 18, they had gone through it three other times with my brothers. Plus, I'm probably not as likeable as my son is, so they may have been pushing me out the front door.

I hope my son calls me more than I called my parents back then. I think I was too busy pretending to be grown to take time to call home as often as I hope my son calls me.

Come to think of it, I'm still busy pretending to be grown. Maybe I should call my parents now. I bet if I ask them to borrow money it will make them feel needed. I wonder how much I could get them to give me.

Ah, the things we do for our parents.

Taking what the garden gives

This year's summer garden is coming to an end, sadly.

Each year we try to get a little more food from our land than the year before. We were very blessed this year.

A buddy of mine drove his tractor over in spring and tilled us a much larger garden to work with than we normally have.

It's neat to see which vegetable will thrive each year. I don't know what makes one particular vegetable do so well one year then not so well the next year.

One year, we had so many cucumbers we were able to pickle some for winter. Last year, zucchini was bountiful. If you have never had lasagna with zucchini instead of pasta, you should try it. We loved it.

This year, our big winner has been okra. As of today, our okra stalks are well over 7 feet tall and still producing. We have jars of pickled okra, along with several bags already frozen.

It also looks like we may have a good harvest of figs here in the next few weeks.

Our honeybees are less than a hundred yards away from the garden. Just having them on our property tripled the garden yield – not to mention all that delicious honey they make.

This year, we planted a kaffir lime tree, two pecan trees and two persimmon trees. Hopefully they will take a liking to their new home.

I say "we" a lot while talking about our garden, but truth be told, my wife is the brains behind this operation. I wish I knew a 10th of what she knows about how to grow plants. I am fascinated with getting food from the land, but she is knowledgeable.

She won't fool with the honeybees, so I do have something around here I can make a claim on.

We are going to attempt a winter garden for the first time this year but are waiting for our summer garden to quit giving us food before we clear it out.

It's amazing to watch the circle of life Mother Nature has provided for us. The chickens help us make compost, which feeds the garden. The chickens then get many of the garden scraps in return.

We try to take what the land gives us and are constantly learning and trying new things. Which reminds me – we have found a ton of muscadine vines growing up trees on our property, but very few muscadines. We are trying to train some to run on a trellis so hopefully we can take advantage of one more thing the land is trying to give us.

If anyone has any knowledge on how to harness muscadines for harvest, please feel free to drop me an email (listed below). I would be forever grateful.

*If you are looking for something to do tonight, consider coming to the Newnan town square for the Fall Art Walk. I will be down at the Newnan Times-Herald trying to sell my book for a grossly inflated price ($10). Many of the other writers for the paper will be there with more reasonably priced books – and art – as well. I have friends who will be selling their art in other spots on the square, along with friends who own shops on the square. Support downtown... Newnan, not Atlanta.

Dealing with extraordinary circumstances

I think, at my best, I am an ordinary man who sometimes deals with extraordinary circumstances. William Halsey was probably right when he said what he said lo those many years ago.

With that being said, there are many times I find myself in awe of the people with whom I work.

One night, I found myself en route to a suicide threat call. A man was threatening to shoot himself and he had the loaded gun to do so.

The first deputy got on scene and made contact with the man. He ended up standing less than two feet to the right of the gentleman. The guy had his gun in his right hand, sitting in his lap. I was standing directly behind the man's right shoulder, with a third deputy standing to my left.

A hundred yards away, stood a SWAT medic who I knew and trusted with my life, literally. I am always happy to know the guys in red are on scene with me, and on this night, this man in particular, I didn't have a care in the world knowing he was with us.

As the first deputy spoke with the suicidal man, I watched his right arm. He was holding the gun with his right hand, which was in his lap. I had never stood so close to a man with a loaded gun and had no idea what he was going to do with it. He had to move his right arm only a few inches to get a shot off on my buddy, or himself.

As they talked, I grew increasingly concerned that it was not going to end well. My buddy was actively listening to the man, and showing a great deal of empathy. He spoke calmly to the man, asking him several times to "hand me the gun." The man was never rude, but he was upset and would always reply "no, I think I'm going to hold on to it."

I was playing through every possible scenario in my mind. What I was going to do if he moved his arm toward my buddy? What I was going to do if he moved his arm toward himself?

I thought for a second about trying to jump on the guy's back. I was less than a foot or two away from him. But my buddy was in a much more dangerous position than I was in. I didn't want to make a move he wasn't expecting and we were not in a position to make eye contact with each other.

The only thing I knew for certain was that we were not in a position to act, but only to react. This man was calling the shots and we would only have a millisecond to react to whatever he might decide to do.

I don't know how long they talked. It was more than five minutes but less than 10 minutes, if I had to guess. In moments like that I'm thinking your internal clock probably isn't worried about the time.

But out of the blue, after much protest, the man handed the gun to my buddy. Just like that, it was over. Now we could get him the help he needed.

As we were walking back to our cars, our Major keyed up the radio and said "good job." This was the middle of the night. My buddy was surprised Major was on the radio that time of the night. I told him anytime he keyed up the radio, no matter what time of the night, to always assume Major was listening.

Reason #957 I say I work for the best agency, with the most amazing coworkers, during the best generation of policing ever.

On the set of a T.V. show

So I'm sitting on a side job for a popular TV show filmed in the area.

I have never seen an episode of it, but I think almost everyone else on earth has. This is the third or fourth time I have worked security for this particular show as they film. They pay well, and the catering trucks are off-the-charts delicious.

I don't know how anyone within a five-mile radius of these catering trucks can keep a "famished look." I guess that's a testament to the actors' skill.

The guys I work with have told me one of the main stars rode by on a motorcycle the last time I worked this gig. And I just saw a lady who I was told is one of the main stars.

I don't speak to them, and they don't speak to me. It seems to be the arrangement everyone prefers.

My job usually has me either blocking traffic or something that leaves me closer to the crew than the actors. These are some of the kindest people on earth. They are accommodating and friendly and all around great people to be around.

My duties seldom put me anywhere near the actors, though according to my friends who have met them and had their pictures taken with them, they are as friendly as the crew.

Not only am I the only person I know who has never seen an episode, I might be the only person I know who doesn't have a picture of me and one of the actors trying to shop around town.

I am amazed as I look out over the parking lot at just how many people this show employs. I'm sure some are transient, but the vast majority must be local folk. It's shocking how many cars are in the lot and how many people are here running around doing whatever they do.

I know all shows eventually end, and that this one has had a good run already. But I really hope it runs for many more years, to keep all these people working. This is a big deal for our area.

I always assume when I am working this show, or any of the other movies I have worked, that the right person is going to see me and realize how they need a chubby, bald, deputy-looking type and demand I get in front of the camera.

That has not happened yet. So far, they seem more interested in the traffic-blocking skills I can provide and less interested in my rugged good looks and acting chops.

It's their loss, I figure.

While most of everything this industry brings to the area is hugely positive, there is one potential drawback that could be devastating.

I don't know how many people are moving here from the left side of the country to work in the industry, but the thought of Georgia turning from a red state to a blue state frightens me.

"Y'allywood" sounds cute and has a nice ring to it. "Georgiafornia" sounds horrifying. To me anyway.

Gone too soon

On our first day of Mandate (Police Academy), the lieutenant over training stood up in front of the class that morning and sectioned off a portion of the large white board that covered the front wall.

He told us that section of the board would be reserved for the names of officers killed in the line of duty during our time at the school. He told us, whether we believed him or not, we would use that much of the board to list the names.

I looked at the size of the reserved space, and I did not believe him.

Every morning, we were to check the "Officer Down Memorial Page" and if there was a new name, someone would read up on the officer so he/she could stand in front of the room and tell the class about that person before writing their name on the board.

Some mornings there would be no new names to be added to the board. Some days there would be more than one. If memory serves me correctly, one morning we had five classmates lined up in front of the class to each talk about a fallen officer.

Five officers. One morning.

Unfortunately, the lieutenant was correct on that first day. We did fill up that section of the white board with the names of fallen officers over the course of our mandate. It was unbelievable to me then, and it's unbelievable to me now, that so many officers' names went up on that board in such a short amount of time.

Earlier this week, a South Carolina officer was killed while trying to serve a search warrant. Six other officers were shot and injured during the same incident.

The fallen officer had just received his 30-year pin with his department.

As of this writing, there have been 113 line of duty deaths this year. That's roughly 12 per month.

Men and women – 113 of them –woke up, went to work and never came home. And they weren't just officers. They were fathers and mothers, sons and daughters, brothers and sisters. There is a human being behind every badge.

To those who respect the job we do, 113 heroes have died this year. To those who do not respect the job we do, 113 people "signed up for that."

But to their loved ones, their son or daughter went to work and died doing their job. Their father or mother died at work. Their brother or sister died at work.

I remember the day I was given my badge. I stared at it. I took pictures of it. I tried different angles, with different effects. They are still saved on my phone. I am more proud of earning that badge than most things I have ever done in my life. To this day I am proud of that badge. It's beautiful to me.

But my family doesn't care about that badge. I hope that doesn't come across as a slight- it's not meant to be. To my family, I'm just me. To our families, we are just us.

"Greater love has no one than this: to lay down one's life for one's friends." John 15:13

113 heroes, gone too soon.

Redefining obesity

I had an angio screening done yesterday.

My employer provided it, free of charge, for anyone over 40.

I wish more employers did things like this. You have to assume if just one employee found out they had an issue that could be corrected early, it would save the company money in the long run.

I come from a long line of bypass surgeries and inserted stints. I think the Nix family crest is a probably fancy looking clogged artery.

Luckily for me, as of yesterday, I am all clear. So either I am still a little but too young to be an official member of the Nix cardiac clan, or I am a testament to the health benefits of a diet high in black coffee, red meat, real butter and fresh eggs. Time will tell, I suppose.

The one down spot on my scan is that I am officially obese. I am six feet tall and weigh 230-ish pounds. I get that I could stand to lose a few pounds, but I think obese might be a tad bit of a statistical overreaction.

Healthdata.org has estimated 160 million Americans are either overweight or obese. Last year, Time magazine claimed 40 percent of Americans are obese.

I know I may not be as much muscle as I like to pretend I am as I am peacocking around the gym, but maybe it's time to see if we can't find a better method for defining obesity. One which takes more than just height and weight into consideration.

We have enough information at our disposal to know being thin does not equal being healthy. No more than being pleasantly plump – as I like to consider myself – equals being unhealthy.

How fast can you run a mile? Can you bench press your body weight? I think numbers like that are more indicative of someone's health than how their weight is proportional to their height.

Maybe if insurance companies started giving discounts to people who could hit certain achievements like that, people would start putting more effort into their health. Throw in a one percent discount for every mile you can walk in one hour and see how many people find a treadmill that year.

I know nothing about how insurance works, so take this column for what it's worth.

I am lucky. Not only does my employer do things like offer free angio screening, they also offer gym fee reimbursement. It's in their best interest for me to be as healthy as possible. It's another step in the right direction that hopefully saves everyone money in the long run, while also giving me as many years as possible on this earth.

While I'm in the subject of changing how we define things, I would beg anyone to come up with a more realistic definition for what a "serving size" is. The amount of servings I get versus the amount of servings the label says I should get are usually drastically different.

Of course, if I stuck to the current proper serving size, maybe I wouldn't be obese.

The man with the urn

I saw a photo making the rounds on the internet the other day.

It was a picture of an elderly man sitting at a restaurant table. The table was set nicely, it was definitely not a fast food restaurant.

Across from the man was an urn. I did not notice it at first glance.

So I went from assuming this man was out at a romantic dinner with his wife to realizing he was sitting at a dinner table with, presumably, his wife's ashes.

Only after I noticed the urn did I notice there was only food on the plate in front of the man.

It may have been their favorite restaurant on what was their anniversary. Or, maybe it was Valentine's Day. I don't know.

What I do know is I don't want to have that dinner date. I guess that means I would rather my wife be the one stuck having that dinner.

That probably makes me selfish, but I can do selfish. I've done it more times than I'd care to admit. I'm not certain I could do lonely as easily as I do selfish.

She is a lot stronger than I am anyway.

But we are both currently living, so one of us is going to be faced with that solo dinner. With her lung problems and my current profession, someone may want to start placing bets.

That picture is still in my mind. It has been since I saw it. I dwell on things, whether I want to or not.

I picture myself sitting at that table across from an urn. I think about how many times I've been impatient, or rude to her. All the arguments we have had over things don't seem like good things to be arguing about once you've seen a picture of a man having dinner with an urn.

I don't want to sit at that dinner table and wish I had done a better job of letting her know how special she was, or how lucky I was she chose to share a last name with me.

Hopefully it will be a long time before either of us faces the prospect of such a sad meal.

Hopefully we will remember, daily, to not take the moments we are given with those we love for granted.

writer's note: after reading the above column, my mother called the house and told me to never write about something like this again.

**writer's note follow-up: I have not written about something like this again*

Flu season is upon us

My dear ol' pappy, who is a man known for being full of one-liners and wisdom… or something, would always tell us: "Believe half of what you see and none of what you hear."

At the risk of bringing up a polarizing subject, it's flu shot season.

I can search online and find some very convincing articles on how bad flu shots are for you. I have read a list of ingredients in the shot that I don't necessarily want in my body. I have also read the flu shot doesn't even cover most strands of the flu.

I believe both those claims.

I can immediately turn around and find just as many, and as convincing, articles on how good the flu shot is for you.

I believe the claims in those articles, as well.

I have friends who swear by the shot. I have friends who swear by not getting the shot. They are all just as adamant as the next as to why their particular opinion is the correct one. They have, so far, all survived every flu season they have encountered.

I don't get the shot. I got it one time many years ago, and felt terrible for the few days that followed. So I just don't get it. My wife has to get a flu shot and a pneumonia shot every year. That's by order of her pulmonary specialist. She has lung issues that make both shots necessary.

The twist to this story is as follows, I got the flu last year. I came down with it on Christmas morning. I had always assumed I had had the flu a time or two in my life. It turns out, what I must have had was a fever and a cough during flu season.

It is only after you have had the flu that you can determine you have never had the flu before. I did not know pain like that existed. It hurt me to lay perfectly still. And I laid as perfectly still as possible for about 36 hours if I remember correctly.

I'm not exaggerating this for "man cold" purposes. I am as guilty as every other man on the planet. I will milk a runny nose for all it's worth. But this flu I am talking about was legit. It hurt. Every muscle, bone and joint in my body- for days.

I never want to feel that pain again. It was agonizing. But does the flu shot really only cover a few of the many strands of flu viruses in any given year? If so, I'll take my chances. I made it 42 years and have only came down with one flu.

Now the people who are at high risk age groups, I understand. The really old or the really young, it might be worth it for them. I don't know.

We live in an age where there is, literally, a world full of knowledge at our fingertips, and I never know what to believe, no matter how credible the source would appear.

Believe half of what you see, none of what you hear... or only what fits your already-formed opinion of what you read.

Mama Nix

My son is at the age where he likes to hang with his buddies. If he is like me, he will never outgrow that stage.

Most weekends there are at least three 17-year-old guys at our house. They all arrive sometime Friday after school then leave sometime of either Saturday or Sunday.

They are good kids. I'm relieved to know he keeps good company.

I'm also relieved they all enjoy hanging at the house, because I would much prefer them to be at our house than my son at their house. I like a noisy house. I can't imagine many good memories were made in an empty house.

I am reminded to my childhood home always being full of people when I was growing up. Of course, thinking back to how small that house was, it wouldn't have taken many people not named Nix to fill it up.

Nonetheless, my brothers and I kept it filled up buddies almost daily. We were very lucky to have parents very welcoming to our friends.

To this day, I will get random messages asking if I remember something my father either said or did back then. If you've ever met him, you would understand why I usually do remember whatever is being asked.

My mother was a mom to many more kids than just me and my brothers. If she had a nickel for every time one of our buddies called her "Mama Nix," she could afford a new house on the beach.

Of course, she would take all the nickel money, skip the beach and just give it all to her kids and grandkids. I should point out, in recent years, she has been called "Nanny Nix" as many times as she was ever called "Mama Nix."

I have watched my brother and sister-in-law do the same thing with my nephew's friends. I'm pretty sure I've even heard a few of them call my sister-in-law "Mama Nix" as well.

My nephew's buddies come to family vacations, birthdays and holidays just like they are part of the family. Because they are.

If you're a Southern woman and the only kids who ever called you "Mama" are the kids you birthed, then something is wrong.

There is no better woman on earth than a Southern woman. Who else could put up with a Southern man? My wife might not be "Southern-born," unless she was born in south Cambodia, but she was raised in the South.

I've never heard her say "bless your heart" but I'll put her cornbread up against anyone but my mom and my aunt.

I'll know she's really made it in life when I hear one of the kid's friends call her "Mama Nix."

I may be biased, but I think the world would be a much better place if everyone had a "Mama Nix" in their life at some point.

On second thought, there is no bias. It's a fact. Here's to all the Mama Nixes, and all the other Southern women who are mom to whoever their kids bring home.

Shop local this season

Maryann Bonk is a local artist and good friend of mine. She can usually be found at the spring and fall Art Walks in Newnan, painting on the square. Her work typically also can be found year-round on the square.

Though I can't draw a stick figure, I fancy myself an art snob. I love her paintings. In a chaotic world, she is somehow able to capture peace and put it on paper, if that makes sense. Peace on a paper. If she ever uses that as a slogan, I want a kickback.

Adam Montgomery is another buddy of mine. We work together. When I mentioned to someone at work that I wanted to get into honeybees, they told me to contact him.

He rode up to the office and sat down with me and told me everything I needed to buy to start off. After making sure I had everything I needed, he even found a hive of bees for me to buy to start my new venture.

Over the past few years, he has been available to answer any dumb question I might have about keeping bees. And believe me, I can come up with some dumb questions.

He has an abundance of honey this year still available for sale. His honey has won awards.

In addition to honey, he can make European mounts from any deer you might get this hunting season. I've seen his work – it's top-notch.

Soon, everyone will be looking to buy gifts for their loved ones. There is no need to go fight the mobs on Black Friday to buy something everyone else is trying to buy.

Look around at your friends. You may be able to pick up something no one else on earth has.

I only listed two of my friends here, but I could have filled this newspaper with talented people, living right beside us, making one-of-a-kind things.

I have two knives that were hand-forged a few miles up the road from my house, in Raymond. Not many people can say that.

These knives are unlike any other knives I have ever had. Sharp as a razor and built to last a lifetime – or two. I will pass mine down to my kids. They will last.

No matter how many other knives are ever made, the ones I have are one-of-a-kind. I like that.

One last thing to mention before we enter shopping season: All a gift card does is take currency that is good anywhere and turn it into a card that is only good at one store.

Shop local if you can. The talent and the quality is there.

An unsuccessful hunt

I had an unsuccessful hunt yesterday.

That extends my current tally to every hunt I have ever been on.

I grew up in Union City and didn't find myself out in the woods much as a kid, so I was late to the hunting game. This is my third season trying.

I figure most people who are reading this fall into two different categories: those who have hunted successfully and those who have never hunted at all.

Since that puts me in a unique position, I thought I would describe to everyone what an unsuccessful hunt is.

I wake up somewhere around 4 a.m. and enjoy a cup or two of black coffee, the only way God intended coffee to be drunk.

I leave the house around 5 a.m. to ensure I get into the woods at least 30 minutes before the sun comes up. The walk from the truck to the hunting stand is not an aspect to gloss over, as walking in the quiet darkness is a level peacefulness I don't often find.

I would guess it's anywhere from a half mile to a mile from my truck to the stand.

Assuming I have remembered to bring a flashlight with me, I spend most of that walk hoping the flashlight has enough battery to not have me walking in total darkness.

Once I make it to the stand and climb up, I sit in darkness as the outline of the trees start coming into sight. I can't describe how quiet it is or how you can hear so much all at the same time.

I love listening to and watching the world wake up, whether it's on the beach or in the woods. On the beach there is the constant sound of the ocean. In the woods there is a silence where a squirrel walking on leaves can sound like a monster buck.

As darkness slowly turns into dawn, my eyes will start picking up things on the ground. I convince myself I see a deer standing there, just waiting for the sun to come up enough for me to get a good look at it.

The harder I look at it, the more convinced I am it's a deer. The sun can't come up quickly enough for this deer to come into plain sight for me.

Much like the last time I hunted, once the sun has finished its takeover of the peaceful darkness, I realize I have been staring at a bush or something else that is not a deer at all.

In daylight, I'm not even sure how it ever looked like a deer to begin with.

Hopefully someday I will be able to describe how a successful hunt feels. Until then, I am more than happy to experience an unsuccessful hunt as often as possible.

Putting the correct foot forward

OCD is distressing. It's not a personality quirk. It's 24 hours a day and it's distressing.

I have dealt with it for as far back as I can remember, and have come to terms with the fact that I will deal with it until I die.

It's like that analogy of the duck swimming in water- looking peaceful on top of the water, while underneath its legs are kicking like crazy. That's how I imagine my brain. 100 miles per hour, all day every day.

I could fill up months' worth of columns devoted to how it affects me and rituals I do throughout any given day, but that's no fun.

I thought instead I would tell a story about how it has affected my wife. As if she didn't have to put up with enough already by just being married to me.

Once when our son was just a wee lad, my parents were coming down to pick him up to take him to church. It was not uncommon for them to do so.

On this particular day, they had arrived and we were all sitting in the living room. My wife was putting his shoes on so they could leave when she put his left shoe on first.

To 99.9% of the population, that's not a big deal. To me, it was terrifying.

You're supposed to put your right shoe on first. I just assumed everyone knew this, but I was wrong. There is no way on earth you can leave the house having put your left shoe on first. How could she be so reckless with our child's safety?

That's what was running through my mind. I don't remember what I said to relay all my internal strife to her.

I vividly remember the look on my parent's, and my wife's, faces when they realized how genuinely horrified I was about this shoe predicament.

Thankfully for me, and my son's well-being, she took his left shoe off and put his right shoe on first. You know, the way God intended.

It's one of the many times she has humored me. I know things like that are illogical. I am thankful she looks past the ridiculousness of it all and goes with the flow for me.

I know me surviving my day is not contingent on whether or not I put my right shoe on first.

With that being said, I would never in a million years dream of putting my left shoe on first. No way, no how.

Point of light (Amberstrong)

George H.W. Bush died Saturday. One of the main things I'll always remember about him was his challenge to everyone to be a "point of light."

He wrote that "points of light are the soul of America. They are ordinary people who reach beyond themselves to touch the lives of those in need, bringing hope and opportunity, care and friendship."

A friend of mine from high school also died on Saturday. As timing would have it, I was waiting in my patrol car to lead a funeral procession across town when I found out about her passing. There were tears being shed in the lead car too, on that one.

I last saw her a few months ago. It's never a good thing when a pulmonary specialist gives you his personal cell phone number. She and my wife shared the same lung doctor, and were both in that unfortunate health position to have his personal cell phone number when they needed to reach him after hours.

One weekend, my wife found herself having an issue with her lungs that couldn't wait until Monday morning "business hours" to address.

We tried to contact her lung doctor, but weren't having any luck. I knew my friend shared the same doctor so I sent her a message telling her about our situation and asking what she thought we should do.

It turned out, what my wife needed, my friend had. So within an hour or two, we were meeting her and her husband so she could help my wife make it to Monday morning.

She had never met my wife before that day. But anyone who knows her knows that didn't stop her from acting as if they were long lost friends catching up after years of not being in touch.

As with everyone who was lucky enough to meet her, my wife instantly thought the world of her.

I don't know how she faced her medical issues with the strength and good spirits that she did.

She was the perfect example of how we should live life. She was exactly who President Bush wrote about when he described what a "point of light" should be.

I hope her children always know how many people saw her as a "point of light."

Church... what a dump!

Yeah, I said it.

I don't remember the last time I went to church, but it's been years. I visited one this past Sunday, and let me tell you, it was a real dump.

I went to Buffington Road Christian Church in College Park for several years, many years ago. That's where I met my wife, as a matter of fact. We were married in that church.

We fell out of church a long time ago and just never went back. No major incident happened, we just quit going.

Deep down, I've always missed being part of a church. I've missed that feeling of peace.

I've always wanted to find Les Shell preaching at Buffington Road, like the old days. It's an impossible task. Neither Les Shell nor Buffington Road Christian Church are around anymore.

Last week, however, I met this engaging Preacher man at a Christmas parade and after speaking with him and the youth pastor, decided I wanted to visit this church.

Sunday morning came and we walked in the sanctuary and chose a pew with no one else on it. It was a Baptist Church we were visiting so we made sure not to pick a spot on the back row. Surely, those seats are all taken.

It may have been years since I've been in a church, but I know how the seating goes. Members have their spots, and I was hoping not to start out at this church with some guy pointing at me as he nudges his wife and says "Hey, they're in our seat. Where do we sit now?"

The church was having their Christmas musical program, so the service was presented by the choir.

We had made it about half way through the service when I realized what a dump this church was.

The choir was singing "O Holy Night" which happens to be my favorite Christmas song.*

(*Side note: John Berry's version is the best version ever.)

For several years, I have been carrying stress and worry. It's a heavy load, both physically and mentally.

Everything is stressful. Work is stressful. Raising children is stressful. Trying to make ends meet is stressful. It's easy to get overwhelmed.

But about halfway through that song, I realized I felt pretty good. I wasn't worried about which bills would go unpaid this month. I wasn't thinking about any promotions at work.

I was just at ease. Being at ease has never been an easy task for me. But I was at ease in the moment. Calm.

I felt as if a literal weight had been taken off my chest. It's hard to describe, but I honestly felt physically lighter.

I had come into that church and dumped at least some the turmoil I constantly carry inside me off inside that building.

And I don't think a single person in that sanctuary minded. I don't know how many were there dumping their turmoil, and how many were there helping people like me unload.

Maybe everyone is a little bit of both.

If you don't get the feeling you're at a dump when you're at church, maybe you should try a different one out. It's a good feeling, I tell ya.

I'm not telling you how you should spend your Sunday. That's on you. I'm just telling you how I spent last Sunday and how I felt. And how I can't wait to go back.

And an unintended upside for me, since we came a few weeks before Christmas is if someone shows up at the Christmas service and sits in our spot I'll be able to nudge my wife and whisper "Hey, they're in our spot. Where do we sit now?"

Comfort Zones

I don't like public speaking. I think most people can relate.

It's a skill I'd like to get better at for both personal and professional reasons.

The only way I figure I'll improve on this particular skill set is to practice this particular skill set, no matter how far out of my comfort zone it may take me.

So when a teacher friend of mine asked if I would come speak to her senior classes I told her I would.

Not only would I be speaking in front of a couple of senior classes, my son was going to be one of the seniors in that class. So if I froze up or made a fool of myself, I would be doing so in front of him and everyone he goes to school with daily.

I asked two friends of mine if they would be so kind as to speak to the seniors with me. They are both also in public safety. Each one has many more years of experience than I, so the kids should be in good hands even if I never uttered a word. They both immediately agreed to help out.

The day arrives when we are to speak at the school. I'm beginning to think that maybe a classroom full of high school seniors, one of which is my child, might not have been the best audience to work on my fear of public speaking with.

Everything ended up being perfectly fine. I opened up the talk. I'm sure I turned red and stammered my way through my brief introduction. I assume I wasn't too embarrassing, my son didn't ask the teacher for the hall pass as I spoke. He was sitting on the back row, as far away as he could get from me though.

Soon after my introduction, I turned to floor over to my friends who spoke, then we had an open discussion with the students, which went well, by all accounts.

I went out of my comfort zone and came back with, hopefully, an improved skill. Life is lived and skilled ads sharpened outside of a comfort zone. That's been my experience anyway.

I'm hoping for more opportunities to speak in public. I am far from smooth or comfortable. But I'm better than I was at the beginning of this column, so that's progress.

And as my profession continues to shows me, going outside of your comfort zone, with people you love and trust, is the only way to do business.

I am thankful for the two friends who didn't hesitate when I asked to come speak. They were helping the students by sharing their experiences. They were helping me just by being there beside me, as they always seem to be when I need them.

New Year's Lunch

My family has gathered up at my parents' house every day for the past few days. Family and food are what make this one of my favorite times of year.

Judging from meal portions we've eaten in that span, we are probably each up around five pounds.

We have all inherited my mother's philosophy on cooking. If you figure 10 people are coming to eat, cook enough food for 25.

It was over one of these Christmastime gatherings that we learned of some pretty distressing news. News that could very well spoil New Years Day, and possibly all of 2019.

It seems there is a shortage of collard greens.

This may not be as frightening to everyone else as it is the Nix clan, but we take New Year's Day collards as serious as we take Thanksgiving turkey and my aunt's coconut cake on Christmas Eve.

You don't get the rounded Nix physique without being serious about the groceries you throw down your throat.

I can't remember ever eating a New Year's Day meal without a huge portion of collard greens.

It might not be the best-smelling dish while it's boiling, but the finished product, doused in pepper sauce and topped with cornbread, more than makes up for the unpleasant cooking odor.

I've been told my entire life that eating collards on New Year's Day brings dollar bills in the coming year. I have a lifetime lack of dollar bills to refute that claim.

I will also eat my fair share of black-eyed peas January 1st, though I have never had any real abundance of coins to get me by any given year, either.

If collards are supposed to bring dollars, and the peas are supposed to bring change, I wonder what the gigantic bowl of mash potatoes is supposed to bring.

Maybe the carbs represented there bring a year full of post-meal naps.

I'd buy that explanation before I bought either of the money superstitions. That is, if I ever had any extra dollars or change laying around.

But what really rounds out the Nix New Year's Day lunch is hog jowl.

It takes a special food to take honors over collards, cornbread and mashed potatoes, and hog jowl is deliciously special enough to do so.

My parents have ordered 40 pounds of hog jowl this year. Forty pounds. And there will not be very much at all left to eat on January 2nd.

If you have never had hog jowl, the best way I can describe it is to say it's like bacon's big brother. It's got a little bit more attitude than bacon and if you aren't careful when you mess with it, you may end up missing a tooth or two.

Eating copious amounts of hog jowl is a good way to let the new year know that, even though you may never have any extra dollar bills or pocket change, you won't let being broke get in the way of eating one of the finest cuts of meat known to man.